Walter Chalmers Smith

North Country Folk

Walter Chalmers Smith

North Country Folk

ISBN/EAN: 9783744775519

Printed in Europe, USA, Canada, Australia, Japan

Cover: Foto ©Thomas Meinert / pixelio.de

More available books at **www.hansebooks.com**

NORTH COUNTRY FOLK

*By the AUTHOR OF "OLRIG GRANGE," "HILDA,"
"KILDROSTAN," &c.*

PUBLISHED BY
JAMES MACLEHOSE AND SONS, GLASGOW.

MACMILLAN AND CO., LONDON.

London, . . . *Hamilton, Adams and Co.*
Cambridge, . . . *Macmillan and Bowes.*
Edinburgh, . . . *Douglas and Foulis.*

MDCCCLXXXVIII.

NORTH COUNTRY FOLK

BY
WALTER C. SMITH

Glasgow
JAMES MACLEHOSE & SONS
PUBLISHERS TO THE UNIVERSITY

1888

Originally published in April 1883.
Uniform Edition, 1888.

Inscribed

To my Friend,

Professor John Stuart Blackie,

Dear to all his Countrymen,

And most dear

To those who know him best.

CONTENTS.

	PAGE
WEE CURLY POW,	1
DR. LINKLETTER'S SCHOLAR,	34
DICK DALGLEISH,	53
LOST AND WON,	69
THE MAD EARL,	81
PROVOST CHIVAS,	106
MORGANA,	125
MRS. COVENTRY,	136
MOTHER AND STEP-MOTHER,	143
BAILIE BUTTERS AND YOUNG DINWOODIE,	147
DEACON DORAT'S STORY,	159
THE POETASTER,	169
PARISH PASTORS,	176
DR. BOYACK,	178
DEAN DUFFUS,	183
THE REV. RICHARD RULE,	190

	PAGE
AMORY HILL,	198
MISS BELLA JAPP,	210
THE VILLAGE PHILOSOPHER,	217
ALTNACRAIG,	220
COBAIRDY,	225
DONALD TOSHACH,	231
IONA,	239
THE CRY OF THE MAIDEN SHAREHOLDERS,	243
A CRY FROM THE MERSE,	246
A REMONSTRANCE FROM THE MERSE,	249
IN MEMORIAM—DR. JOHN BROWN,	252

Wee Curly Pow.

Off with you, wee Curly Pow; off, little kitten, to bed;
You'll not leave a beard on my chin, and you'll not leave a hair on my head,
If you kiss me and touzle me so; there; already it's bald on the crown,
And once it was thatched like a hay stack, the furziest head in the town.
Will I kiss you in bed to-night? Of course, I will, when you're asleep;
And you'll know it because you will dream of angels that stand and weep
O'er chatterboxes that won't go to bed when they ought to go,

And all these angels have beards that are three days
    old or so—
You do not believe that angels ever have beards;
    they fly
With beautiful wings, and their hair is like sunbeams
    up in the sky?
Oh, you're a learned wee maidie; but yet it may well
    be true
That I do not know about angels so well, my
    darling, as you.
There; off with you now; that's the last, the very
    last kiss you shall get,
And mind you, I will not be cheated, you're twenty
    at least, in my debt.

Draw your chair nearer the fire, friend; there is a
    storm in the air:
Hark! how the sea is moaning: God help the fisher-
    folk there
Out in their crazy old boats, for we shall have wind
    and snow
Driving from the north-east soon, if aught of the
    weather I know.
But the bickering log is pleasant, with the collie
    coiled on the rug,

And the kettle there on the hob to brew us a steaming mug.
What! no more brewing to-night? you would rather be still and brood?
So be it; and well; I can guess what has started your thinking mood.

You are wondering who that child is, and what she can be to me,
A dull old bachelor here in the farm-house down by the sea?
A niece, a cousin perhaps? you had no ill thoughts in your head:
If you had, you would only have thought what scores of people have said.
Nay, no apology; none is needed: I've learnt to bear
Harder suspicion than yours, sir, and never to turn a hair.
I've nothing to be ashamed of; if all the truth were known,
It may even go to my credit, when God and I reckon alone;
Only that, good folk tell me, is hardly an orthodox thought:—

Not that I care, in the least, sir, whether it be so
 or not;
People here are afraid to utter a word out of
 joint,
But for me, I am far and away beyond our minister's
 point:
Trouble has taught me, like Job, that sometimes
 the veriest lies
Get them a hiding beneath the well-ordered words
 of the wise;
And wee Curly Pow is my darling, wee Curly Pow
 is my bliss!
God gave me her in my sorrow, as one seals love
 with a kiss.

Oh, my Lizzie! my Lizzie! yet Lizzie never was
 mine,
Except as the thing that we love is ours by a right
 divine,
Except as the beauty of nature is his who has eyes
 to see,
Though not an acre he owns, nor so much as a bush
 or a tree;
And so my Lizzie is mine by the love which for her I
 bore,

Yea, a possession which nothing can rob me of
　　evermore.

Perhaps I should tell you the story: it is an old
　　one now,
And it calls up things that are best left sleeping, I
　　think; for they grow
Into hard thoughts when you stir them, mudding
　　your life again,
Just when it seems to be settling, and clearing off
　　sorrow and pain.
No matter; you have a right to know what it all
　　may mean,
For you are my friend, and a friend should see
　　what there is to be seen:
One should have no dark closets locked in his heart
　　to hide
Aught from the wife of his bosom, or from the friend
　　he has tried.

It is some ten years now since Lizzie—Pet's mother,
　　you know—
Came·to be servant at Blavick—that's the next farm
　　as you go
Land-ward, maybe a mile hence; perched on a bit
　　of a hill

Down which brattles the brook that drives the wheel of our mill;
Worst farmed land hereabout, all scarred like a pock-pitted face
Grey and unwholesome to look at; poor soil it is at the best,
But starved too, for money is scarce there, and work not so pleasant as rest.
Anyhow Lizzie came there, at Lammas some ten years past,
As bonny a lass as you'd see, sir, and clever and merry and chaste;
At kirk or at market you could not meet such another, nor find
At kirn or wedding to dance with a partner so to your mind,
Always so tidy and neat, and always as blithe as a bird,
With a ready laugh for your joke, and as ready a word for your word.

Blavick's wife was a slut—or she had been, for now she was dead,
And Lizzie, you see, had come to keep house for him in her stead—
Sluttish women are mostly fat, of a rosy tint,

But she was a black-a-viced person, bony and hard
    as flint :
Yet such a house as she kept, sir! pigs and hens
    and dogs
Littered the floors along with the milk pails, peats,
    and logs ;
Hard to pick your way through, for the place was
    dark with smoke,
And that had been hard to breathe, but mostly a
    window was broke.
Oh the dust on the settle! oh the soot on the wall!
And oh the dirt in the dairy, that was the worst
    of all !
I wondered how she could live in it, not at all
    that she died ;
But for long years she had lost all a woman's
    natural pride.
Blavick himself was always lounging about the place,
A hulking lump of a man, with a huge expanse of
    face :
And if talk could have done it, all would soon have
    come right.
How he did talk, to be sure, all through the day
    and the night !
Maundering on about limes and guanos, rotation of
    crops,

Soils and subsoils, and ploughs, and the makers of
    them and their shops,
And all the new-fangled ways! but none of the old-
    fashioned work
Ever he put his hands to: there was not a rake or
    a fork,
Plough or harrow that was not broken and out of
    repair
Just when they needed it most, and waste was
    everywhere.

But Lizzie began at once to make everything nice
    and clean,
To put everything in the house in its place where
    it should have been;
Pity the pig that ventured to grunt inside of her
    door!
Pity the hen that entered where it used to cackle
    before!
The kitchen was like a parlour, none of them dared
    to tread
With mucky shoes on her earth-floor; for she had
    a tongue in her head.
Women need to be able to scourge a fool with
    speech;

That is their only weapon to punish him or to
    teach ;
And it was worth while hearing her hit them off,
    one by one,
Every phrase just a picture, lit up with a touch of
    fun,
Making them all, shame-faced, to do her bidding at
    once,
Till, at the last, she needed no more than a hasty
    glance.

Blavick used to be hateful; but now it grew pleasant
    to me,
At first, I hardly knew why, but just that I liked
    to see
The change that Lizzie had wrought; for that I
    would sit for hours
And hear old Blavick's chatter, as if it were sweet
    as the flowers.
Many a time when I went out just to look over a
    field,
And see how the corn was ripening, or guess at the
    turnip yield ;
Many a time when I came away from the thronging
    fair,

Pleading I must go home for the task that I had to do there;
Many a time when I left for the kirk on the Sabbath day,
It was not the kirk I went to, for Blavick was in my way:
Somehow or other, something was always drawing me there,
As the tide runs after the moon—and oh but my moon was fair!
Then I knew that I loved her—loved her with all my heart,
As only a strong man can whose love is his strongest part.
She was only a servant maiden, but oh she was my queen:
She was only a cottar's daughter, and I was the farmer of Plein;
My fathers had been here, sir, for five generations back,
And never a lease ran out but the laird would renew the tack,
For they had money to farm with, and they could farm with skill,
And never a lease ran out, but the land looked richer still.

Yet she seemed high above me—ever so high above!
It never came into my head that I honoured her
    with my love;
Nay, but she was my moon, my chaste and beautiful
    moon,
And I but the panting tide that followed her syne
    and soon;
She was so bright, quick-witted, and I so dull and
    slow,
She high up in the heaven, and I on the earth
    below.
Folk said that I might do better; I thought, if she'd
    condescend
To smile on me, I would follow her on to the
    wide world's end.

But there was one at Blavick—and he too the worst
    of the lot,
Partly a horse-couping black-leg, partly, moreover,
    a sot;
Fain to look like a jockey, wearing a jaunty hat;
Some folk called him good-looking,—I am not a judge
    of that—
But in his eye was a hot moist leer, and he had a chin
That dropt inside of his necktie, and a hard and tight-
    drawn skin.

Other folk called him clever, but I should say only
    smart—
I call a man smart when his head does not feel
    the want of a heart,
And works best when it has laid the conscience high
    on the shelf,
Regarding not God or man, and caring for none
    but himself.

What is it women can see in men assured and
    bold,
That they give their warm true hearts to hearts that
    are false and cold?
That they give their pure hearts up to men that
    are foul with sin,
Nor shrink from the outward taint, nor dread what
    is hidden within?
I never could comprehend how such things come
    to be,
And now it is more than ever a mystery grown
    to me.
That Blavick's son was a scamp, sir, as all the
    country knew:
You could read it plain in his face, he neither was
    manly nor true;

He ought to have been ashamed to speak to an honest maid,
And she too ought to have known the weapon with which she played,
Ought to have known the fellow would lead her a devil's dance.
But now there was no getting speech of her; hardly I met her once;
Always you saw them together; he went with her to the kirk,
Chatted with her at the milking, sat with her in the mirk;
In harvest she was his bandster; she raked for him at the hay;
And wherever you happened to meet her, he never was far away.
Ay! and he made her tryste him beside the " Dancing cairn,"
Although she had heard the story of Bessie Lusk and her bairn;
But she said it was all a lie; the sheriff had let him go,
And Bessie had fallen asleep, and died in the drifting snow,
And even the minister found no fault that he could blame,
And it was wicked to rob a man of his honest name.

All this I saw going on, and yet like a fool, one day—
Every man plays the fool, I suppose, sir, once in a way—
Finding her by herself, I asked her to be my wife;
And when she had said me nay, ere I turned to my lonely life,
Partly because I loved her, and partly because I feared
What might happen, if things went on as they now appeared,
I warned her of him, as none but a fool would have thought to do.
Of course, she blazed up fiercely: there was not a word of it true;
'Twas gossip of wicked people, and some folk's meaner spite;
And she would believe in him now, though I proved it clear as the light;
And she would hold to him now, and sink with him or swim.—
I felt there was something grand in her womanly faith in him,
Felt too that I had been little—at least, that I must look small,
Though I said no more than the truth, and had not said nearly it all;

But then I should just have taken mine answer, and
 gone my way.—
A weary way now it was, sir, of lifeless work all day,
And brooding by night o'er the fire, and eating my
 heart like a fool,
Till things grew over my mind, like the weeds in a
 standing pool,
And I scarce knew what I was doing, or heeded a
 word that was said,
Going to kirk and market, and never once turning
 my head,
Doing my job of business, doing my bit of prayer,
With a changeless thought in my heart, and a
 changeless aching there.
People, I daresay, wondered why I sat brooding
 alone;
What did it matter to me? I let them go wondering
 on.
I hated the clash of the market, the glee of the
 curling rink,
And the rough jokes of the smithy, the ale-house
 too and its drink;
Yea, and I hated my life so brightened once by her
 smile,
So haloed and hallowed to me by the dream of her
 love for a while,

For now it had all gone dark, and I did not seem to mind
What the clouds might be gathering, or what might be in the wind.
Maybe, sir, you have known, now, a feeling something like that,
When there's nothing you fear or wish for, it is all so stale and flat,
Tasteless and dry as a rush-pith you chew, and you don't know why—
It's a bad way to be found in if the devil should hap' to come by.

So the spring passed with the tender green of the sticky leaves,
The songs of the mating birds, and the swallows' nest in the eaves;
So too the glory of summer with the smell of clover and bean,
The hawthorn white in the hedge, and the daisies white on the green;
And autumn also went with its wealth of well-stooked corn,
And the kine that low for the milk-pail duly at even and morn.

Nature passed through her changes, but I was still
    the same :
I fished ne'er the pool for the trout, and I fired not
    a shot at the game :
People were wedded and buried, but I was not
    there to see,
At harvest-homes the lasses might none of them
    dance with me.
There was nothing I heeded, except to put cash in
    the bank—
Not that I cared for that either, at least not much ;
    but I thank
Heaven that I grew not a miserly churl as I might
    have done,
But for my wee Curly Pow, and her laugh like the
    blink of the sun.

But there ; I am going too fast, there was not a
    Curly Pow yet ;
But I never can think of those days without thinking
    too of my pet,
And what she has saved me from, and how I am
    in her debt :
Perhaps she was given me for this, to keep me from
    being a churl,

For my heart was set on the gold, until it was set on the girl.
Well; one evening that winter—it had been snowing all day,
And now with the dry small drift the wind was making rough play,
Rolling it low o'er the earth, and tossing it high in the air,
And whirling it over the cliffs to toss up the white foam there.
Not a night to be out in; but I thought I must go and look
After a hirsel of sheep that were pasturing down by the brook
In the hollow there where the rocks have opened to let it through;
There the pasture is good, sir, and the pools for trouting too.
So; I had seen to the sheep, and was fighting my way again
Home through the blinding drift that smote with a stinging pain,
When something flitted close by me, and moaned as it made for the shore
Just where the rocks stand up, two hundred feet and more,
Out of the wild wan water, with only a narrow ledge,

Here and there, where the sea gulls build, and their
 nestlings fledge.
Even in quiet weather it is perilous walking there,
At night, for the cracks and fissures you come upon
 unaware,
Where the waves rush in so madly, tossing the white
 foam high :
But on a night like this one who was not wishing to die
Would have kept far from the wind-swept cliffs,
 and the drifting snow,
And the loud roar of the waves that were plunging
 down below.

What was it smote my heart that the form which
 dimly fell
White on my eyes through the snow was the girl
 I had loved so well?
Why was I sure that I heard her moan, though the
 raving wind
Shrieked till my ears were as deaf as my eyes with
 the drift were blind?
Heaven only knows, for I had no reason to think
 that she
Was out of the house that night, or near to the
 rocks or me :
Yet I was certain of it, as if it had been revealed

Clear by the word of the Lord, and with miracle signed and sealed.
So in a moment I rushed off after the fading form
Into the pathless night that was dark with the blinding storm;
And not five yards from the cliff I passed her with labouring breath,
And stood in front of her there, stood between her and death.
Pallid she was as a ghost, with a wild gleam in her eye,
Gleam of the madness that drove her out that evening to die:
Ah, poor soul! so lately rich in a full-blooded life,
And merry as bird in the summer, or bee when the clover is rife,
Glowing and singing, and laughing all through the work of the day,
Ah! what anguish had broken a spirit so blithe and gay?
What cruel wrong had dethroned a reason so sharp and clear
That had not a moping doubt, and felt not a shadowy fear?
" What did I mean? Let her pass. And what right had I to ask

Whither she went or why? And, forsooth, it was
   not my task
To be her keeper," she said. It was not a time
   for speech:
Vain in the tumult of feeling to order your words
   and preach:
So then I tore off my plaid, and swathed her in
   it, ere she knew,
And lifted her up in my arms, and strode through
   the tempest that blew
Wilder, fiercer than ever; and after struggling a while,
She lay as one dead on my bosom for most part
   there of a mile.
Ah! was it only thus I should bring my love to my
   home?
Only thus to my bosom now was she ever to come?
No gay bridal for us, no Kirk's blessing or bells?
But a dead weight on my arm, and something of
   sorrow that tells.
How I got home, I wot not: but I strode on,
   slow or swift,
With a great black fear on my heart as I fought
   with the wind and drift.

My mother was living then; and when I laid
   down my load

There on the sofa beside her, saying that Woman
 and God
Must see to the rest of this gear; she gave me a
 sudden glance,
With plainly a question in it, and something of
 doubt, perchance,
As if she would say, 'There's something wrong here;
 can it be you
Has wrought this evil, my son? God help me if
 that be true."
Then, " Look you, mother," I said, " there has been
 villainy here,
Double-damned villainy, sure, and the truth of it
 yet shall appear,
Ay! if I pluck his heart out to get at the secret
 within ;—
Oh! I would have given my life to save her from
 sorrow and sin.
But something has to be done, or after all she will die.
Is she living? I thought that I heard a shivering sigh.
She was making straight for the sea, when I found
 her close to the brink
Of the Kittywake Rock.—Ah! that was a moan
 of life, I think ;
Can I do anything, mother? If he were here now !
 Well,

It would only be doing God's work to hurl the
    villain to Hell."
Then she: "Leave God Himself to do His own
    work, my son;
Vengeance is His, and surely, if slowly, His judg-
    ments are done:
Do not the thing that you ought not, for so our
    worst sorrows are wrought,
And sorrow, I fear me, will come yet from doing
    this thing that ye ought.
But happen what may, ye did right: only now you
    must saddle and ride;
This will need Doctor's skill. 'Tis a wild night,
    lad," she cried.
"And you are down-hearted and cold; and yet it is
    better for you
Than sitting, helpless, at home, to have something
    set you to do.
So let not your horse's hoofs tarry, but mind the
    bridge and the shore,
And speed him as fast as you may, or death will
    be here before."

Four miles' ride to the village, but the wind was
    then on my back;

Four miles home with a gale in our faces that did not slack
Once for a moment; a while to saddle the Doctor's brute,
And get him into his shoes as he growled at a gouty foot:
Yet we were back in the hour; ay, that was the staunchest mare
Ever stood in my stable, or ate from the manger there.
But we were not in time—Wee Curly Pow came that night,
Came from the sin and the shame to me as an angel of light.—
Strange that out of such evil such a blessing should rise,
That from the very heart-breaking came the heart-healing likewise.
But Lizzie was taken from me; she never looked on her child,
The troubled unhappy soul sped forth in the tempest wild,
Seeking to hide her with God, where hiding is found alone;
And oh so still as she lay now, trouble and tempest gone!

Mother looked sadly at me, and gravely the Doctor too

Hinted that tongues would be clacking or ever the
    day was through,
That the farmers of Plein had been always men of
    an honoured name
Which never till now had been smirched with a
    shadow of guilt or blame.
What was there now to smirch it? Drily he smiled
    at that,
Turned up his eyebrows, and said that day would
    tell me what:
Meanwhile my heart within me was wroth at the
    villain's deed;
Meanwhile my heart was breaking to have failed her
    now in her need;
For I had loved her truly, and now I was left alone;
And oh so still as she lay there, trouble and tempest
    gone!

Not long had I to wait for what their foreboding
    feared;
One day quietly passed—the lull ere the storm
    appeared;
But on the next, like fire among burning ricks, it ran;
It was told by every woman, believed by every man,
How I had played the deceiver, how I had brought
    disgrace

On the good name that was honoured o'er every
    name in the place;
How Blavick's son had been blinded, and all his
    people beguiled;
And how in her shame she had fled to the father of
    her child;
And they say that he carried her home a mile
    through the drifting snow;
And who could have ever believed that Plein would
    have acted so?
I laughed as the tale was told, but I tried to be
    still and mute,
For the grief was more than the wrath, so the
    story had time to root,
And you cannot fight with a rumour which nobody
    stands to quite.
For that is like hitting at shadows and beating the
    air at night.

Then it was that I found a blessing in Curly Pow:
She was all of my love that remained, all of Lizzie
    that I had now.
Every day she would lie for hours and hours on my
    knee:
I was but an uncouth nurse, but she learnt to trust
    in me;

And I got to love her somehow, and it would have
 broken my heart
Had anything happened on earth to make me and
 the baby part.
They might think what thoughts they pleased, they
 might say of me what they list,
When she crowed up into my face, and learned to
 look up and be kissed.
It was all of my love that remained, it was all of
 my Lizzie I had,
And Lizzie had been my all. But, of course, they
 said everything bad.

Of course, they said everything bad. The minister
 once came in,
And vowed at my own fireside if I did not confess
 the sin
He must cut me off from the Church; he was
 sorry, but what could he do?
Some one, I said, must confess, for that sin has
 been done is true—
Sin of the shamefulest kind, and covered with
 perjuring lies,
Sin that came nigh to murder, no art can ever
 disguise,

Sin malignant that shifted its guilt on the innocent too,
Sin that took up ill reports, and spread the false
    word for the true,
Verily sin all round. But for me I have nought to
    confess,
Save that in pity I saved a life in its great distress.
But maybe the Priest and Levite blamed the
    Samaritan's sin
For binding the traveller's wounds, and bringing
    him home to his inn;
He saved an enemy's life, and it cost him money
    to do it;
It was not a prudent act, for only the Lord God
    knew it.
Who then did it? he asked. Enquire at your
    Elder's son,
The horse-couping scoundrel,—it's not the first of
    these jobs he has done;
You've had him through hands before. Yes! he
    swears he is not to blame?
But when you had last to deal with him, did he
    not swear the same?
Yet he was guilty, you know, and was held to
    have doubly sinned,
And sat on the stool of repentance, and stared at
    the girls and grinned.

What do you think, sir? It strikes me that did
 not do him any good;
And who is the better because her babe is unchris-
 tened? or would
Be worse if it were baptised? It is nothing, of
 course, to me;
But if it is right that the babe who has sinned no
 sin should be
Brought to the water of God, then why should this
 little one bide
Like one who inherits a shame, while her father has
 none to hide?
See, I will hold her up before all the folk if you will,
I'll take all the vows on myself which I'll faithfully
 strive to fulfil,
Will toil for her, pray for her, teach her to walk
 in the way undefiled;
Though there's not one drop of the Plein blood
 flows in the veins of the child.
I cannot lie even to get you to bless the babe that
 I love;
It is not my child; but it's God's; and its name too
 is written above.

He was mightily scandalised, and flung right out of
 the house:

But I did not heed him; I knelt there down by
    my wee little mouse—
She was not my Curly Pow yet, for she had not a
    hair on her head,
But she always got some pretty name as I took
    her upstairs to her bed,
As Mousie, or Birdie, or Daisie, or anything dainty
    or sweet,
Or the Star or the Song of my life, or my Lamb
    with its tender bleat—
So I knelt, and prayed to the Father to help me
    to train her for Him,
Since worse than orphan she was, and I felt that
    my eyes grew dim,
While I sought for the better baptism that she
    might be pure and good,
As no Kirk water could make her. And then in
    a happier mood
We crowed and played there together, until it was
    time for bed;
Where I lay and dreamt of my Lizzie, who lay with
    the silent dead.

Well; yes, the house now was lonely; but that I did
    not much mind:

People must go their own way; and for me I was never inclined
To mix with the folk round about here, who mostly have nothing to say
Save about cattle and crops and the prices on market day.
Not to pleasure the like of them should my ways be changed:
So they might do as they listed; and most of them were estranged.
But I always had wee Curly Pow to help me to carry it through,
And life is as happy to-day as on ever a day that I knew.
Ay! neighbours leave us alone, and the Kirk has cast us away,
And every day of the week is as still as the Sabbath day:
Worse thing they had not to do; it was all the length they could go.
Baby don't mind, but at first I felt it a terrible blow
To be shut from the table of God, to be held as an outcast man,
To be looked at askance like a branded sinner and publican.

I went still to Church for a time, and sat on the
    square Plein pew,
And heard the old Psalms, and the prayers, and
    bits of the sermon too,
Meanwhile I wept like a child, as I thought of the
    happier days
When father and mother and all of us loved the
    old Kirk and its ways.
But ere long I stayed here at home; for I found
    more of God in the child,
As I looked on her sweet pure face no shadow of
    sin had defiled;
My Sundays were better with her than there where
    my neighbours gloomed,
As the minister preached at me sometimes, and I
    sat and fretted and fumed.
I don't say it's right, sir; but God seems nearer
    me here now than there,
My thoughts are sweeter and better with wee
    Curly Pow in her chair,
As we read in the old Book together, and kneel
    for a brief word of prayer.

What came of the horse-couping blackguard? I
    never cared much to know:

For I found it was best for myself just to let the
    thought of him go
Out of my mind altogether; it was a dead fly, do
    you see?
Spoiling the ointment of course—working no good,
    sir, in me.
He left the place by and by, with the constable
    hard on his track,
Making it certain enough he would not be in haste
    to come back:
Then there were rumours about him; he had been
    killed, they said,
In the Bull's Run affair, and found in the field 'mong
    the dead;
But others averred he was caught horse-stealing,
    and lynched on a tree.
Bah! he is out of the way, sir, and that is the
    best thing for me:
There was nothing I dreaded so much as to meet
    him some evening alone
Where I met poor Lizzie that night. Ay, it's well
    that the fellow is gone.

Dr. Linkletter's Scholar.

I was his master; and from me
He learnt at a sitting his A B C:
And step by step I led him through
    Grammar and History, Latin and Greek,
And the science of Form and Number too,
    And Rhetoric that he might fitly speak
As only the well-trained orator can,
For speech is the noblest gift of man;
But speech that is not by the laws and books
Is but as the cawing of jays and rooks,
Or the meaningless babble of running brooks:
And from the first it was plain to me
What his *role* in the world must be.

It was my mind that was stamped on his,
   When his was soft as the melted wax;
Yet it was not wax, but gold; and it is
   Strong too and sharp, as the woodman's axe,
To hew him a way through the tangled bush,
And also to smite his foe at a push—
Just the mind that is sure to win
Whatever the tussle it may be in,
For in this world they only tell
Who learn to hit out straight and well.
Therefore I follow his proud success,
   Day by day, as he rises higher,
Read what he says in the public Press,
   And note what the critics all admire;
And this bit and that which the whole world praises
For its lofty thought, or its happy phrases,
Or its insight clear, or the counsel wise
That in its large suggestion lies—
I could not have said it so well as he,
But I know there is something in it of me;
I could not have worked out so perfect a thought,
But I gave him at first the true key-note;
For I was his master, and from me
He learnt, as I told you, his A B C.

Ah! sir, only to think that you

Had not the fitting words at command
To utter the thought that you felt was true;
   And what it may grow in a master's hand!
At times, I can hardly detect the seed,
   When it blossoms out in the perfect flower,
For it had been only a trifling weed
   If left to ripen by sun and shower
In the poor soil of a mind like mine:
Yet the germ of it all was there, I know,
Though only he could have made it grow
Into a glory so divine.
Wonderful, sir, that genius should
Transform your thought, like its natural food,
And breathe into it a life so rich
   The author of it shall hardly find
What of it now is his, and which
   First smote the spark from the glowing mind!

A chit of a thing when he came to me;
   No shears had ever yet come over his head,
And his mother could hardly bear to see
   The golden curls which at last were shed,
That he might be like the rest of the boys
   Who jeered at him, till she polled his hair.—
She kept it among her treasured joys,
   Wrapt up in her marriage lines with care.

And I felt with her, as I must confess :
  He was so beautiful before,
So touched with a sweet and tender grace;
And now we had made him commonplace,
  Like the louts that were playing about the door.
A little ago he seemed just a child,
Thoughtful yet bidable, gentle and mild,
My little Nazarite, five years old,
With his great black eyes, and his hair unpolled;
And I felt he would be my Samson yet,
  Not for his brute strength and clumsy sport,
But for a fine and arrowy wit
  Quick to reason, and keen to retort,
And for a memory that forgot
Of all you might teach him never a jot.
Already I saw what he was to be,
  When he shook the curls of his golden hair,
And now as the small face looked at me,
  I thought, ah! what if his strength was there?
And I felt my eyes like her's grow dim,
He was so changed when we gazed at him.
That was a foolish thought, but love
  Makes all of us foolish now and then,
And he who thinks he is far above
  Such things is the foolishest among men;
Fond may be foolish, yet love is wise,

They call it blind, but the seeing eyes
See best by the light in the heart that lies.

Oh but our work went merrily now,
Blithe as the birds that sing on the bough,
For all the lore of the ancient times
    Came with as natural ease to him
As song to the thrush on the stately limes
    Piping aloud in the evening dim.
It was not work, it was liker play,
Teaching my pupil day by day;
Yet sometimes it was dreadful too,
    He kept such a resolute grip of all
    The gods and heroes mythical,
They were all so real to him and true,
And all their loves and hates he knew,
Better than what went on around
Among the boys on the playing ground;
And in his innocence he would talk
Of Jove and Leda in our walk,
And of the foam-born beautiful One,
And the myths of the all-embracing Sun.
But all is pure to the pure in heart,
And chaste as the marble of highest Art.

Ah! sir, you cannot know what it is,

How it wears the patience down to the bone
To toil through a summer day like this,
   Sharpening fools on the grinding stone,
While stolid or sullen they grow by fits,
And nothing will put an edge on their wits;
We have to be pedants and too precise,
Or nothing would flourish but sloth and vice.
But oh the joy! when you chance to find
One who can answer to all your mind,
Who hungers for learning, as hawk for its prey,
And never forgets a word you say—
A bright young soul to be trained with skill,
Ready to take what shape you will,
Believing, loving, intent to know,
And clear as a mirror the truth to show,
But not like a mirror to let it go.
That was a gladness he gave to me
From the day that I taught him his A B C.

Only once had I ever seen
   Such another, who so combined
Memory, fancy, and reason keen;
And he from the first had always been
   Sickly in body, though strong in mind.
Ah the sorrow I had for him,
   As he wasted slow with an inward fire,

And his eye grew brighter, as mine grew dim
   With the dying of hope in a deep desire!
A beautiful spirit! and when he parted
   From the shrunken form, and the aching pain,
I said, as I sat down broken-hearted,
   That I never should love, as I had, again,
Spending my life on him day by day,
Only to steal his life away.
For I ought to have noted the hectic streak,
When first it flushed on his pallid cheek,
And I—I had only worked him still
Because he worked with so ready a will,
And his mother, I kept the truth from her—
And what, if I had been his murderer?

Yet here was another like the first,
   But brighter still; and now if he
Were also to die, I should be accursed
   Of all proud mothers that heard of me.
   Therefore I said, it shall not be;
We will not always be poring on books,
We will not study with sickly looks;
We will go up to the breezy hills,
   And scent the smell of the old pinewood;
Or down where the sea-spray flies, and fills
   The air with a breath that is also good.

It is stupid indeed to be spending hours
    Only seeking for vulgar health;
But then we can gather the lore of flowers,
    And drink in the wonder of nature's wealth,
And fight off Death with the weeds and shells,
And the strong, rich life in the sea that dwells.
So rarely a day then came and went,
    But we heard the plash of the rushing wave;
And often a day on the hills was spent,
    Where the mountain ash or the pine trees brave
The mist and the cloud and the storm-wind's shock,
With roots clawed fast to the grey-brown rock.
I watched if a fire ever burned in his eye,
    I watched if a flush ever dyed his cheek;
Not his mother herself would have watched as I;
    Yet I only watched him; I did not speak;
For thinking of health may bring disease,
And I did but talk of the hills and trees,
And the bright sea-pools, and the running brooks,
And the dainty gulls, and the cawing rooks,
And how they were better than musty books.
That was not true; but you have to hide
Your thoughts from the eager ones at your side.

So passed the school-years, gathering in
    Harvest of wisdom from the wise,

Harvest of pictures for the eyes,
Harvest of song for the heart within—
Harvest richer than all before,
   For it was not books that we read alone,
   But God's handwriting on earth and stone
Penned by Him in the days of yore,
Though it's only now we begin to spell
The sacred writing, and read it well.
Oh so glad were those years to me!
   Oh so fruitful of freshest thought!
Watching the gull or the guillemot,
Or searching the rock-pools by the sea,
Or learning from the nest-building swallows,
   Or noting the woodman and his craft,
   As he felled the pine trees, and bound the raft,
Or poled it down through the rushing shallows!
At first, I grudged the hours it took,
At first, I sighed for the half-read book,
And carried its thoughts about with me,
Until I found that we could not see
The world without for the world within,
Nor gather the health we were there to win.
So the books and the maps were laid aside
That we might look forth open-eyed,
As Homer did, on the world wide.
And good are the pictures still, I find,
Then hung in the chambers of the mind.

What a career was his at college!
   Never the like of it seen before,
Since Crichton, Admirable for knowledge,
   Startled the schools with his wondrous lore.
Not Faust was a defter spirit than he
In Letters and Arts and Philosophy;
Medals, scholarships, honours poured
Down on his head with one accord,
And yet the small head was not turned,
But only for yet more learning burned.
People would glance at the Honours' list,
   And say, "Is there nothing he cannot do?"
For ne'er at the head of it was he missed;
   His name was the first that came in view
In Classics and Logic and Rhetoric too,
Which are the things that the wise of old,
More than all others, received to hold.
Yet some folk, envious, hinted that such
Prodigies rarely came to much.
I knew better. I worked with him
Night after night, till the lamp grew dim,
Night after night, till the day would break:
   For I said, He will carry to many lands
My name like Ascham's, and for his sake
I too of fame shall yet partake;
   For I am the clock-work, he the hands.

Oh, I was proud of him; who but he?
For was he not also a part of me?
Of course, he was more than I; yet so
What I too might have been, he would show.
And when at length he was capped, the town
   Gathered to see him, and shout his praises,
As, smothered in prize-books, he sat down,
   And blushed at the Principal's eloquent phrases;
But his mother and I were hid in a nook,
And mingled our silent tears, and shook.

Ah! is there anything leaves no sorrow—
   The mark of the human—on its way,
When the hope that brightened the looked-for morrow
   Drifts past at length into yesterday?
Well, well! it is idle to moralize,
   Wasting breath upon empty sighs;
And we have ourselves, no doubt, to blame,
   When bubbles burst we have fondly blown;
And if you have properly played the game,
   Shall you grieve that one of the tricks is gone,
Which you hoped to win with the cards you had?
Or vow that your partner's play was bad?
I was foolish and vain, sir; for I thought
   I was filling his mind like an empty bottle,
When we read Justinian now, and wrought

At the politics, too, of Aristotle.
But he was not a vessel that I could fill;
He was a man with his own strong will,
And I was wrong when I took it ill.

Why is it people smile at me
   In a pitying, patronizing way?—
They've always done it, even when they
Were learning with my eyes to see
The beauty of classic verse or prose:—
   They tried to hide it, but yet I saw.
What can it be? I am not like those
   Beautiful youths, I know, who draw
All hearts to them by their witching look:
   In a drawing-room now I lose my head,
Till I get in a corner, and find a book,
   And lose myself in its thoughts instead.
It is true, I am awkward in company,
And blush if a lady but speaks to me,
And never do find the right word to say,
And my legs or arms are in my way,
And I've no small talk, nor a spark of wit,
And my laugh is not mirthful—can that be it?
Well, well; I am nothing, and ne'er shall be,
Unless my pupils interpret me;
Just like a language few will take

The pains to learn, though it hide a store
Of precious wisdom and curious lore,
And those who learn it a name will make.
But I hoped that he would esteem it more.

Yet his mother herself would sometimes say,
  He has no heart; he is only brain;
There is nothing he loves in a perfect way,
  There is none that he would not grieve and pain
To gain his end. And I also felt,
  Though he had no passion of youthful vice,
  But was ever as pure and cold as ice,
Yet was it ice that nought could melt;
And he never was young like other boys,
Nor made them his friends, nor loved their joys.
He was fain to argue and to dispute,
  Even when he saw that he was wrong;
It was idle his arguments to refute,
  For when he was beaten by reasons strong,
He would ride away on a jest or two,
In the triumph of laughter mocking you.
At the lowly in heart too he would sneer,
  And the simple in heart he held for fools,
And there were times when he made me fear
  He cared for us only as his tools.
Yet maybe we led him, ourselves, to think

That only for him did we keep our lamps trim,
That all our wells were for him to drink,
  And all existed only for him.
And oh, what a mind he had! what power!
  What subtlest insight to detect
  The hidden analogies few suspect!
As the wild bee travels from flower to flower,
And brings quick life to the barren seed,
  So would he bring from far afield
  What made the commonest things to yield
Undreamt of meaning, and life indeed.

So it came at last that, in gown and wig,
  I heard him plead in a fitting cause.
How the words rolled from him round and big!
  Not Tully himself more versed in the laws
Of Rhetoric, how to turn and wind
  Round judge or jury, and win their ear,
Then flash a metaphor into their mind,
  Or a stroke of wit that they smile to hear,
And, when he has got them well in hand,
Close with a peroration grand—
Or touching, if that is the vein most fit;
  But, with our British mind, I know
Hard reasoning and a harder hit
  Will often farther than pathos go,

Or pictures of clients in stricken woe.
He hit the nail on the head, I saw:
Not once did he miss a point of Law,
Or fail the heart of the case to seize,
Or to persuade and rouse and please:
Nothing was showy or juvenile,
　Nothing merely for ornament;
Every word was in perfect style,
　Every plea to the marrow went,
　Clenched with a telling precedent.—
Oh, what a gift is that, to stand
　Before the majesty of the Law,
And hold your argument clear in hand,
　And state the matter without a flaw!
I had studied the case myself at night,
And seen it, I reckoned, as clear as light:
But I felt, as I heard him pleading now,
The cold sweat beading upon my brow,
And there was a ringing in my brain,
And all was dark, till he made it plain.
I could not have spoken a word for awe
Of the ermined majesty of the Law.

Now when he finished, the Judge looked down,
　And complimented his able friend:
The Bar had done, he was free to own,

All that the Bar could to defend
A weighty cause in a weighty way,
And to fulfil the hope which they,
And all who knew of his honours won
   In other fields, had formed of him.
So the grave Judge. When he had done,
   My head went round, and my eyes grew dim,
And something I said—I know not well
What it was,—but a silence fell
On all the court; and I seemed to see
A little boy at his A B C,
Sitting thoughtfully at my knee.

Of course, it was wrong in me to go
In the hour of his triumph thus, and show
My thread-bare coat, and my withered face
At such a time, and in such a place;
Though it's true my coat was thin and bare
That he might be garmented fitly there.
But it cut me, at first, to the quick, when he
Turned with a freezing look from me—
Maybe, I had said something wild;
My head was dazed when I thought of the child
And what he had grown with the help of me,
And what in the future he yet might be :—
Still it was wrong, and I see it now,

So to intrude with empty and vain
Thoughts of myself; and I ought to bow
  To the fit rebuke, though it gave me pain
    As I crept away home in the dripping rain.
Of course, he loves me, I surely know it,
But that was not the right time to show it;
And nobody likes, in the hour of his pride,
To have shabby old friends creeping up to his side.

What a brain he has for clearness and power!
  What a grasp of principles and details!
What would take you a year, he will seize in an hour;
  And then his courage too never fails.
He may be Lord High Chancellor yet,
  But he will write as a scholar no less;
(To think that a part of me may be set
    To give law from the woolsack, or teach from
      the press!)
None of your idle poems, or flash
Essays, biographies, tales, or trash,
But solid works for the thoughtful few,
Writ with a golden pen and true.
I know it is in him. I put it there,
And he will bring it out clear and fair,
When legal briefs, and affairs of state
  Slacken enough to give him leisure.—
But that must be soon, for I may not wait

Many more days for the Psalmist's date,
  When years are a burden, and not a pleasure.
Hard, hard he works for the fame he seeks
Through the busy term, and the holiday weeks;
Yet he never is weary, never complains,
Knows nothing of sickness, or aching pains,
Or a wish for rest, or bile-clogged brains.
That is the fruit of our happy days
By the windy shores, and the wooded braes.
Wonderful, wonderful! such a man!
  If he would only, now and then,
  Drop me a hasty scrap of his pen,
When he has leisure to write, and can!
It's hardly reasonable, I know,
In me to be looking for that, although
I spent the wealth of my life on him,
  And all the knowledge of studious years,
And filled his cup as it were to the brim
  With the lore that now in his life appears.
But what of that, sir? And what had I
  Been but a grave to bury it in,
Were it not for the scholar I trained to fly
With the bravest of them that mount up high
  Riches and honours and fame to win?
And he has won them, and shall win yet
The ermined robe, and the coronet,
And a noble name, and mine shall be

Blended with his, too, in history.
And I've thought, now and then, in that coming day,
When they talk of us, they will maybe say
I was the Moses that saw the Lord,
He but the Aaron that gave the word.
But that is when I am vain and proud,
And sit by the fire, and think aloud.
Wondering why he only writes
A scrap to say that he has no time;
And I'm ready to think that is nearly a crime,
As I brood and fret through the long dull nights.
But I ought to be grateful, indeed, that he
Finds even a moment to think of me,
With his hands so full, and his mind so strained,
And the splendid place by his genius gained;
For they say he is not more in request
  At the Courts of Law than in stately Halls,
Where his wit has made him a welcome guest,
  And Beauty swims through its routs and balls.
Ay, ay! and still I am sitting alone
Among the old books by the old hearth-stone.
But I do not grudge him; I only hope,
When his cup is full, he will spill me a drop,
For my work is done, and my days are dim,
And my heart grows thirsty to hear from him,
As the shadows of the Eternal fold
Around my head that is grey and old.

Dick Dalgleish.

Just a mechanic with big, broad head,—
  Carpenter, maybe, or engineer,—
Deft with a skilled hand at winning his bread,
  Scornful of varnish and show and veneer;
Rough-handed, plain-spoken, strong in his youth,
  Loyal to all of his order and craft;
Loudly maintaining the fact and the truth,
  At all pretences as loudly he laughed;
Laughed at quill-drivers, and white-fingered dandies
  Measuring ribbons with yard-stick and tape;
Laughed more at frowsy men doctoring brandies,
  And calling their drugs the pure fruit of the grape:
He slept through the night, and he toiled all the day,
And nothing he drunk but the brook by the way.

Out on a holiday, wholesomely dressed,
   Clean-washed, clean-shirted, his wife by his side,
With a small baby she clasped to her breast,
   And chirped to, and watched with a motherly pride.
Proud of her baby, and proud of her Man,
   All her young face was like sunshine to see :
No sickly vapours had she, nor a wan
   Fine-lady look, but was healthful as he.
How she looked up to him! Who was so clever?
   Who was so good as her Dick? It is true,
He was blunt-spoken, but then he would never
   Harm a poor worm or a fly, if he knew;
And he read everything—science, and plays,
And poems, and all that the newspaper says.

Out on a holiday, sailing down
   The broad clear river that bore away
Thronging crowds from the broiling town
   To the birch-clad hill or the sandy bay;
Shrewdly he glanced at either shore
   Lined with the half-finished skeleton ships,
Spoke of their rigging abaft and afore,
   And what they might do at their trial trips;
Plainly knew all about this one's gearing,
   The other one's engines, paddles, or screw,

And the new methods of working and steering,
  What coal they needed, and what coal could do;
And shrewdly projected a wonderful dream,
Into the future, of iron and steam.

I scarce know why, but I rather took
  To the manly bearing of him, and the fond
Young pride which his wife shewed in every look,
  Than to all the rest, as their ways I conned:
They were mostly broad-cloth citizen folks,
  Each with his newspaper where he read
The markets first, and the price of stocks,
  And what at the bankrupt sittings was said:
They carried their business with them always,
  While their wives were towny and overdressed,
Talked of their city life, and its small ways,
  And dinners and weddings and fashion and taste.
So I took my seat, with a frank good day,
By the big mechanic in homespun grey.

I was fain to speak of his craft and trade,
  But he went rather at first for books:
Did I not think that Darwin made
  A case for the worms as against the rooks?
What had the birds done for earth like these
  Dumb, silent ploughers who made the soil

For rooks to nestle on its high trees,
   And man to live by his sweat and toil?
That was a man, sir, with hardly a rival
   For his power to see, and his grasp of thought;
And as for his doctrine of fit survival,
   That's the new gospel this age has got;
And we must be rid of the drones in the hive,
That the real workers may live and thrive.

They're nearly all drones now on board here to-day;
   Our lads went off with an earlier boat;
But wife, sir, and baby must have their own way,
   And she likes the gentle folks when she's afloat.
It is so, you know, Kate; you're fain now to hear
   The sweet-spoken damsels come praising your child;
And if we went down, you would rather appear
   With respectable folk, pretty-mannered and mild,
Than stand at the judgment with Dick, Tom, and
      Harry
   Not more than half-sobered with gulps of the
      sea—
Oh, how can I say so, when you chose to marry
   Such a blunt working chap, such a rough tyke as me?
That's true; yet you cannot deny it was you
Brought me here with this soft-handed, soft-headed
      crew.

Would you wish me, old girl, now, to be just like these,
  With broad cloth and white linen worn every day,
And to saunter through 'Change for an hour at my ease,
  And call that my work, though it looks so like play?
Their brow never sweats with the work they have done,
  Unless at some queer job that looks rather ill,
And then it is but for the risk that they run,
  When they shuffle the cards for a trial of skill.
Now, I come home at evening, Kate, dirty and weary,
  But my conscience is clean, and my head, too, is clear;
I don't sit, and drink wine, and make the house dreary,
  As some of them do half the days of the year;
I take on no stains from my work or my play,
Which a pail of fresh water will not wash away.

They buy and they sell for the rise or fall,
  When neither a rise nor a fall should be,
Filching a profit still, great or small,
  For the doing of nothing that I can see.

There's a little chap sitting yonder—look!
　He's bulling and bearing all the day long;
And they're fain to glance at his jotting book,
　For they say that his guesses are seldom wrong;
I call him the big flea blood-sucking commerce,
　And these are the little fleas blood-sucking him;
And they live upon us, all our winters and summers—
　Swarms of them, sir—in the handsomest trim,
They make their game, and the stakes are laid,
And they rake in the gold which the workers made.

Yet what have they done for the world by their strokes
　Of betting and hedging? I want to know that.
And who is the happier hearing their jokes?
　And whose life is helped by the jobs they are at?
With their sharp arithmetic they fashion a blade
　That cuts a big slice of our profit away;
And yet they've done nothing for it except trade
　On the folly of some, for which all have to pay!
I used to read Carlyle, and laughed at his "gig-men,"
　And I still like the old fellow's rough tongue a bit;
But he never yet said how the "clothes-men" and "wig-men"
　Must make way at last for the men who are fit.

That's Darwin's discovery; and how can you doubt
These chaps, like the Dodo, are bound to die out?

When you spoke to me first, you were wishing to
    know
  About us, the working men; what our thoughts
    are;
And whereto our strikes and our unions grow;
  And how near the end is, or, maybe, how far.—
Ah, folks are grown curious about us, who once
  Sniffed the grease of our moleskins, and hurried
    them past.
You're not of that sort, I allow; and perchance
  We are crustier, now that our day's come at last,
Than we should be. That comes of the way we've
    been living;
Men trample on man, and they make him a brute;
Though of course we ought all to be taking and giving,
  And keep our good humour and manhood to boot.
But those who have tasted of slight and neglect,
When folk grow too civil, are apt to suspect.

I don't say it's right. But at one time I made
  What was plainly to me a new thing in our line;
A saving of labour to quicken the trade,
  And bring in more wealth than the gold in a mine.

Well, I spoke to the head of our firm; but he turned,
    With a big oath, and bade me go work at my
        tools;
He had heard such tales once till his fingers were
        burned,
    And he found that your workmen-inventors were
        fools.
But afterwards, learning more truly about it,
    Oh, he spoke me so bland, and would fain see
        the thing;
So I brought forth my model—as proud, do not
        doubt it,
    As Kate of her baby there,—and with a swing
Of the big hammer, I dashed it in bits,
Saying, What could come out of a working man's wits?

I had toiled at it, sir, every night for a year,
    So hopeful and happy in seeing my thought
Turned now into iron, and coming out clear,
    At last, through a plain inspiration I got.—
For why should not God inspire minds to invent
    As well as to preach, and be praised for His gift?
Sir, it came like a flash and a thrill that were sent
    In a moment of failure, when I was adrift;
As "the still small voice," which the prophet must
        hearken,

Because it was God's, so the thing came to me,
Like the gladness of light when that failure did
    darken
Around me, and I was as broken as he:
And what is the joy of their gold, and their gain,
To the gladness I had when I saw it all plain?

You think it was childish to waste the ripe fruit
    Of my labour and thought. Not a whit; it's all here
As clear in my head as that day, and to boot
    Some riper thought still that may some time appear.
But I told you this only to show how, in vain,
    Folk think all at once they can heal the huge rent
In our social order where one's heart and brain
    Find seldom the right place for which they were
        meant.—
But why don't I patent the thing I invented?—
    Oh, and rise in the world, as they say, and grow
        rich,
And have a grand house finely papered and painted,
    And mount me a-horseback to land in a ditch,
And dress my good Kate in her sealskin and silk,
And quaff my champagne as it were bottled milk?

Well, I once knew a man with a head-piece to
    think,

 And hands that could work out the thought of
  his head—
It is true that he had a bad weakness for drink,
 And would whimper about it, and wish he were
  dead ;—
But he took to that line, and had everything fine,
 A house in a big square, with lamps at the door,
And carriages, horses, and flunkies, and wine,
 And heaven knows what that he had not before.
But the ladies were shy of his wife; and the
  flunkies—
 The lazy fat rogues, I'd have sweated them well—
At the back of his chair stood, and grinned there
  like monkeys,
 And down in the kitchen they laughed at his bell;
And he had not a moment of comfort or peace,
Till a crash stript him bare as a sheep of its fleece.

No, I'll not take that way, sir; I don't care to rise
 Above my own class—we are happier so.
The Son of the Carpenter now, He was wise
 In the old town of Nazareth long, long ago.
We are not very pious, we workmen, I fear,
 Don't go much to church, but we read about Him ;
And the things that we read are not quite what
  we hear

The minister blow off like froth from the brim
   Of a pot of small beer. Nay, I don't blame the
       preacher ;
It's just what we want that we find in our books;
   As the sun is a painter to some, and a bleacher
       To others; it is as the eye is that looks ;
You open the door to which you have the key,
And I find the message that God meant for me.

But the Carpenter, now, did not care to be great,
   And to ape what the fine Lords of Herod might do,
Nor yet be called Rabbi, and sit in the gate
   As a Judge, or a Parliament man to the Jew.
The fox had his hole, and the bird of the air
   Had its nest; but He had not a roof o'er His
       head,
And heeded not purple and sumptuous fare,
   And borrowed a grave when He lay with the dead.
And this is the gospel I read in the story—
   Though I don't say it mayn't have another to
       you—
The Lord did not seek His own honour and glory,
   But stood by His craftsmen and fishers all through
He held to His class that their ills he might cure
And lift up the head of the needy and poor.

Well, that is our gospel too, that is our Ark,
  Not to rise from our class, but to raise the class
    higher,
Not to take to the nice ways of lawyer or clerk,
  Not to turn from the hammer, the file, and the
    fire ;
But to stand by our order, and stick to our tools,
  And still win our bread by the sweat of our brow,
And to organise labour by Christian-like rules,
  Not that some, but that all may be better than
    now,
May have homes of more comfort, and lives with
    more leisure
To read, and to think, and to well understand,
And to get, like us here now, some holiday pleasure;
  For they do the work that enriches the land.
No ! I don't care to rise for myself, till I see
The rest get a chance, too, of rising with me.

You're a Christian, sir ? So am I, in a way,
  Though some of our fellows, and good fellows
    too,
Have no other gospel or God, as they say,
  Than Man, and what man's brain and fingers
    may do.

I don't go with them, but I reckon my trade
   May be my church too, if the right heart is there,
A-healing the wounds which the selfish have made,
   And helping the helpless their burden to bear.
He is parson and priest, though his apron be leather,
   And he tuck up his shirt sleeves to do his job well,
Whose heart is most loving to sister and brother,
   Most ready to go where the sorrowful dwell,
And to shew to the erring the right way of truth,
And bring them again to the faith of their youth.

Now, the faith of my youth was that Christ would redeem
   The life of the poor from its sorrow and sin,
Would wake up the world from its wealth-loving dream
   To seek the true riches of manhood within,
In wisdom and worth, and the peace which they bring.
   That's the word which I heard from my old mother's lips;
But now it's another guess-song that they sing,
   And the light of her heaven has all suffered eclipse.
Oh, we boast that the poor man may rise in the world,

And we point to his sons who are lords in the
    state,
A-driving in carriages, scented and curled,
  Or making their bow to the gold-stick-in-wait.
And where shall you find, now, a sight so grand,
Except in this truth-loving, Christ-serving land?

Well, well! what rare tricks we do play, to be sure,
  With our conjuring cards, and our thimbles and
    peas!
To think that a God could come here, and endure
  A cross to make lordlings and ladies like these,
And to leave all the rest of His brothers to pine!
  There's your thimble, and Christ in't; but presto!
    begone!
Lo! the devil is there, where the glory divine
  A short while ago sat in sorrow alone!
O blessed the poor—if they only get money;
  And blessed the meek—if they stand to their rights;
And all who are selfish shall have milk and honey,
  For they are the salt of the world and its lights!
Ay! that's the new gospel, I call it, of Gold;
But we working men will hold fast to the old.

Yes, I know we're divided, as other folk are,

And what is yet worse, we are cursed with that
    drink ;
And many are selfish, and some of us mar
    A good cause with bad ways, and some do not
    think ;
And we've blundered, 'tis true, and been wrong now
    and then,
    And done what we should not—as who has not
    done ?
But we'll learn by our failures ; we're only poor men,
    Kept like children till lately, now trying to run ;
And sometimes, of course, we get tript up and
    . tumble ;
    But still on our clouds, lo ! the rainbow is set,
And a light springeth up in the hearts of the humble,
    Will grow to more fulness, and gladden us yet—
But there ! I've been preaching until I have got
A drop in my heart that is bitter and hot.

That's the way with all preaching ; it don't make
    one sweet.
    Where's Kate and the baby ? They'll put me all
    right.
Oh, the ladies are praising its hands and its feet,
    And its mouth and its nose, and its precious
    eyesight !

Well, well ! do you see, sir, that narrow green glen,
  With the strip of dark alders that show where
      the stream
Flows on in its loneliness far from men,
  And ripples, and murmurs like one in a dream?
I speak like a fool, for of course you can't hear it,
  Though I hear it singing away to itself,
Or sobbing at times like a sore troubled spirit,
  Or laughing perhaps as it slides down a shelf;
I was born there, sir; and we're going to try
A week with old mother—Kate and baby and I.

Lost and Won.

BROKEN.

She trusted him with her whole true heart,
  She trusted him as we trust in heaven,
Whatever they said, she took his part,
  And loved with the love to the noblest given.
    Oh, so deep as the water flows!
    Oh, so pure as the lily grows!
    But Love it is deeper and purer than they;
    Well-a-day!

For him she left her father's Hall,
  And the happy life she had prized of old,
And with a light heart turned from all
  Who once had loved her, and now looked cold.
    Oh, so deep, &c.

And by his side she shared his lot,
   And gazed on his face with a tender pride;
Poor they were, yet she murmured not,
   But with a smile would her troubles hide.
     Oh, so deep, &c.

Ah! had she died when her Love was young!
   For she trusted him, and he was not true:
O that she had died ere her heart was wrung!
   For there came a day when this thing she knew.
     Oh, so deep, &c.

There came a day when a beam of light
   Searched his soul, and at length revealed
Heart to heart, and she saw him right,
   And all the lie he had long concealed.
     Oh, so deep, &c.

She read him clear as a printed book,
   And never a word to him she said;
But shot at him only a sorrowful look,
   As her heart sank in her, cold and dead.
     Oh, so deep, &c.

Broken in faith and heart and mind,
   Yet no one knew it but only he,

For she was true to her womankind,
  And no one felt it, but only she.
    Oh, so deep, &c.

She turned her from all joy and mirth,
  In wifely patience silent, pale,
And cared no more for a thing on earth.
  But that dead love of her life to wail.
    Oh, so deep as the river flows!
    Oh, so pure as the lily grows!
    But Love it is deeper and purer than they
    Well-a-day!

PARTED.

Out of his life she passed,
  The one gold-thread that was there;
Out of his life at last
  She dropt with her burden of care —
    How had she ever come there?

He was not worthy of love
  Such as she gave to him;
And yet, like the heaven above,
  She clasped with her light the dim
    World that was dear to him.

How could she so cast away
  The love that was born of God,
The wealth in her heart that lay
  On a man who only trod
    Mean ways that were far from God?

His sorry heart she had taken
  For a nature noble and true,
And slow was her trust to be shaken,
  Though colder ever he grew,
    The closer to him she drew.

And into his life she brought
  Some touches of tender grace,
Some gleams of a nobler thought
  Redeeming its commonplace—
    Had he known his day of grace!

She had been to him like a song,—
  And the song it was silent now—
Or a stream that prattles along
  Where the life-roots feebly grow—
    And what was to come of him now?

For he was selfish and cold,
  For he was earthly and hard,
For in the guerdon of gold
    Only he sought his reward—
      Poor soul, so earthly and hard !

How could she give him her love,
  And he so unworthy of it ?
What were the great gods above
    Thinking of there where they sit,
      When they sent her to fold him in it?

Ah ! the gods know what they do,
  Whether giving or taking away;
They waste no life that is true,
    They lose no game that they play,
      And cast no blessing away.

For as she lay there in death,
  Lo ! for the first time he saw
All her meek love and her faith,
    And there came sorrow and awe
      As its great beauty he saw.

Yea, there came sorrow and awe,
  As the gods entered his life,
And the great word of the Law
  Cut to his heart like a knife,
    Seeing the shame of his life.

And he lay low on the earth,
  When from his side she had passed,
Loathing all gladness and mirth,
  Loathing himself now at last,
    When from his life she had passed;

Stricken in heart, as he thought
  Of the waste of her love and trust,
Of the grace that to him she had brought,
  Of the glory he laid in the dust,
    When he slighted her love and her trust.

STRICKEN.

Ah me! he said, I do not mourn my loss;
  I was not meet for such good company;
Thou all these years didst bear a silent cross,
  And it is right thou shouldst no longer be,
    Comrade to me.

I judge not others; few so bad as I:
  Enough to know my own poor little heart,—
As here in self-abasement now I lie,
  And feel that it is best for thee thou art
    From me apart.

O love! my love! and yet I wonder how
  I dare to call thee love, who was not true:
Yet I did love thee, and I know it now
  Too late, too late, when I can only rue
    My way with you.

I was not always worldly, hard, and cold,
  I can remember yet a better day
When love was dearer to my heart than gold;
  My God, how could I cast it so away?
    Woe worth the day!

Ah me! where now the visions of my youth,
  The nobleness, the glory of its dreams,
Its purpose high, its eager search for truth,
  Its hatred of the thing that only seems,
    And falsely gleams?

Where the fond hope of holy love and pure,
    That, in a cultured home, afar from strife,
With patient service of the meek and poor,
    Reckoned to make a great and perfect life
        With a sweet wife?

Was it all an illusion—but a cloud,
    Sun-painted in the morning, far away,
And filled with lark-songs, by-and-by to shroud
    With mist and drizzle all the dismal day,
        And mud-strewn way?

Nay, but it might have been, it might have been;
    'Twas I that failed, not nature that deceives;
Had I been faithful I had surely seen
    The better hopes, for which my spirit grieves,
        Gathered in sheaves.

They are not false, those golden dreams of youth;
    But we are false to them, and fall away
From their high purpose, following the smooth
    World-lies that win us empty praise and pay,
        And lead astray.

They might have been, ah me! they might have
   been;
And oh the sorrow to look back, and know
They are not, and our life is poor and mean,
   Achieving only loss and empty show,
      And shame and woe.

They might have been? A woful word is this;
   I might have been a nobler truer man,
I might have laid up memories of bliss,—
   She would have helped, but sunless now and wan
      Is life's brief span.

And looking back, I see the morning glory
   Grown dim, and fading 'mid the earthly smoke,
My fond dreams telling now a sorry story
   Of thoughts ill-marshalled, and the battle broke
      Without a stroke.

O heart, that was so rich in noblest wealth
   Of love and joy—to think I slighted thee
O broken heart, erewhile so full of health,
   How in thy grief my bitter shame I see
      God, pity me!

HUMBLED.

Why should I care to live another life,
    When this is done?
I have not made so much of this first spool
That I should crave for other lint or wool
    To be ill-spun:
O heart, my heart, have you not made enough
    Of this poor stuff?

Would I go on for ever, fain to weave
    More of this gear—
More tangled thrums, more broken ends of thought,
More snarled hasps, another hapless knot
    Of sorrow and fear?
An everlasting web of life like this,
    Would that be bliss?

God help me! If I'm only just to do
    As heretofore,
Better into a quiet grave to creep,
And lay me down in peace, and go to sleep
    For evermore:
Or better even right-off to be sent
    For punishment.

Yes! I could find some comfort in the thought
    Of being scourged,
Were there but hope that this defiling sin
Which mars my life, and taints my heart within
    Could so be purged,
And I might live, in virtue of the rod,
    The life in God.

It is a coward heart that shrinks from pain,
    But not from wrong;
Could I but hope to reach a purer air,
God, I would say, lay on, and do not spare;
    Smite hard and strong:
There are no pains that mortal men inherit
    Worse than I merit.

I had a grace that should have made me great;
    I had a love
Which should have made me loving, and I thrust
The gift from me, and clave unto the dust,
    Till from above
God stretched His hand, and took again to heaven
    What He had given.

But oh, if in another truer world
    We yet might meet,

As in the days that seem so long ago,
And I this wretched heart of mine might throw
    Down at her feet,
And say I wronged you, and I was not true
    To God or you!

Yes! I could live for such a day as that
    With patient hope:
Would heaven but grant me opportunity
Of clear repentance which her eye could see,
    Then let me drop
Any where, out of sight, to live no more
    As heretofore.

The Mad Earl.

And that is our Earl—poor fellow! I should not
 have known him a bit,
Had we met on a street: how he's changed to be
 sure! he had never much wit,
But at least he was handsome, and now he is bloated
 and brown as a toad,
And his brains gone to slush, like the snow when
 a thaw comes down on the road.

It is years now since I have seen him, except in
 the woods far away
Pacing alone where the close trees shut out the
 light of the day,
Shunning all speech of man, and still more a
 woman to face;—
Ay, ay! the weird is upon him that has to be
 dree'd by his race.

These grand old families now, there's a story about them all—
A ghost-room, a tragedy somewhere, a writing upon the wall;
Of course they are shy to speak of it, but on a winter night
It's the talk of the cottage fireside in the dusk of the dim rush light.

They tell of the Statesman Earl—'twas he made the house so great—
A shrewd-witted Parliament man, and Councillor high of State—
How shifty and clever he was with the turn o' the tide to swim,
And how when a Bisset or Cheyne died, their lands fell somehow to him.

Folk called him the great lord Spider: yet the small lairds still drew near,
And buzzed about him like flies, for he was the big man here;
And play ran high in those days; you might gamble a good estate
Between the wine and the dawn; and his lordship's luck was great.

That's how the curse came on them—that ne'er
    from his house should depart
A lord who was out of his wits, or a lady who had
    not a heart,
For three generations coming; at least, so the old
    wives said,
But maybe the woes of the house gave rise to the
    weird they read.

Everything must have a reason; every fire once
    had a spark;
And what like the judgment of heaven for clearing
    up things that are dark?
None of his neighbours throve, and none of his
    race had their wits :—
Easy to patch up a tale coming pat to your hand
    so in bits.

Anyhow, certain it is that the Statesman earl had
    a son,
A gallant and gay young soldier, beloved of every
    one,
Till one day his charger stumbled, and they picked
    him up for dead—
Better he had been, for henceforth he never was
    right in the head.

Then followed this one's father; he slobbered a deal
 at his meat—
His tongue was too big for his mouth—and he
 shambled too with his feet;
But he knew the right side of a penny, and looked
 to his farms and woods:
Only nobody saw him at last, and they say he had
 wild-beast moods.

But this Earl Ughtred, he looked right as a man
 could be :
I knew him well as a boy, for he took a rare
 fancy for me,
Chose me to go with him fishing, as well he might,
 for I knew
More about trouting and fly-hooks than idle keepers
 could do.

I was bred, you see, from a child on the bank of
 his choicest brook,
And fished it with crooked pins, when I knew ne'er
 a word of my book,
And my father too could busk you the daintiest
 deadliest flies;
And the young lord saw that I knew the pools
 where the fish would rise.

And many a talk we had as we tramped o'er the hills and the heather,
Or dropped the spoil in the creel, or lunched on the banks together;
And what would he not do for me, when he came to man's estate?
For still he would go off a-fishing, and I must still be his mate.

A fine, frank lad, sir, he was; and he would have done all that he said;
It was not his blame that he did not; but he never was strong in the head;
He had not a turn for books; and he used to have dreamy moods;
But his heart was sound at the core, as the healthiest oak in the woods.

It's true, he turned wildish awhile—as all of his race have done—
He was handsome and wealthy and young, and guidance wise he had none;
I sometimes wonder myself, could I carry a cup so full,
And not spill a drop by the way, but keep my head steady and cool?

By this time his father was dead, but he never had
    been of much good;
Vice was engrained in him, only he did it as cheap
    as he could;
What little mind e'er he had—it never was much
    to be sure—
Had been given to hoarding and hiding the pennies
    he screwed from the poor.

So Ughtred would not be like him, would rather
    be lavish than mean,
And scatter his gold like the best where the nobles
    of England were seen;
Alike open-hearted and handed, had he only the
    brains to know
Among all the ways that were miry where was the
    safe one to go.

Wild, then, he was for a season—forsooth, he must
    bet and race,
Though he scarce knew a horse from a cow, sir,
    unless she had horns to her face;
So the blacklegs got at him early, and sold him
    the weediest screws
Which he backed, of course, at their bidding, till
    he fell in the hands of the Jews.

Then he got frightened, poor fellow, and something or other he did—
I never could make out what—to men of his order forbid;
They did not say it was wicked, but spoke of it as of a shame,
And the great folks pitied his mother, and shook their heads at his name.

That don't go for much with me; for I've lived on their skirts all my days,
And I know that their honour allows them to walk in the doubtfulest ways,
And I know that their honour forbids what conscience does not refuse—
And he never was strong in the head, sir, and he was in the hands of the Jews.

But it touched his mother; who was among us like a sov'reign law;
Her pride was something the people whispered about with awe;
And now to be pitied!—that made her more haughty than ever before,
And she held up her head the higher, and hardened her heart the more.

Then, his sister, the Lady Ion—she just came of
    age that year—
A splendid creature to look at, but also a woman
    to fear,
Features clear-cut as in marble, an eye that was
    bright and cold,
And a perfect seat on the saddle—a rider as cool
    as bold :—

I am his lordship's servant, and it is not for me
    to speak,
But the Book it says that the strong should be
    helpful still to the weak ;
And if all the tales be true that came from the
    big house then,
Better for him had he faced the wrath and the
    scorn of men.

'Twas hard for her, I allow, to have that shadow
    of shame
Cast on her morning sunshine, stigma on her
    proud name ;
But he was the head of the house, though ever so
    weak in his mind,
And they were strong and cruel, who should have
    been strong and kind.

There was a girl that he fancied, sweet as a rose in June,
All other girls in the county were only as stars to her moon,
All other girls in the county were but as weeds by the rose
That in the bloom of its beauty in some stateliest garden grows.

Her fathers were barons here, when the great Earl's house was small
As the stable where their horses stood champing each in his stall;
It is not for me to say how, if certainly ever I knew,
But slowly their acres had dwindled as his lordship's acres grew.

But my lady and Lady Ion, they would not hear of the match;
They mocked at her as a cottar whose door was shut on a latch,
For there was nothing to steal there, but only a wax-doll face
Blooming on bread and milk, and just fit for a milkmaid's place.

Ah! pride, Sir, is hard as flint, and the sparks struck
    from it are hot,
Here and there flying unguided, to burn where
    little you wot;
They hurt not her in the least, but see what they've
    made now of him,
Moping and mooning about here wherever the light
    is dim.

Then came the Colonist girl—that's she who's her
    ladyship now—
That she had her wits about her was writ on her
    sharp little brow;
Pretty and clever enough, with a glittering hard blue
    eye,—
Ay! she would see to herself if her face was not
    wholly a lie.

Colonial manners are frank; she would talk to any
    she met—
Cadger or molecatcher—free, as she walked through
    the dry and the wet,
And oh but she won folk's hearts, for she neither
    was haughty nor shy;
But I liked not the cold blue glitter of steel that
    I saw in her eye.

She thawed the Dowager's frost—like a breath of the
  coming spring,
And toned her speech till it seemed like the songs
  that the spring-birds sing;
What could she see in her now to sweeten her
  manner so,
And make so much of a girl who was hardly a
  lady, you know?

Colonial girls are free, Sir, and Colonial manners
  are frank,
But then Colonial money is good as the gold in
  Bank;
And she had dollars in millions to patch the rents
  he had made
Racing and betting, and learning the way that the
  Hebrews trade.

The Dowager, then, looked sweet, and the Lady Ion
  was bland,
As they led her over the Castle, and showed her
  the goodly land,
And they praised Earl Ughtred to her, and the
  race from which he grew—
They were not clever perhaps, but their hearts were
  good and true.

Meanwhile he mooned about: but would sometimes go fishing with me,
And then he was like himself, and would laugh with a boyish glee,
To hear the birr of the reel, or to land his fish on the bank—
Till he turned him homeward, and then his face looked weary and blank.

Well; one day she came up to me with the daintiest rod and reel,
A casting-line twined round her hat, and hung by her side was a creel,
Boots of porpoise leather, and petticoats not too long,
In trim for a day of sport, and humming an angler's song.

"I want you to take me with you, and show me all how you do;
There's nothing our Earl now cares for, except an outing with you;
Of course, I am fishing for him, and they too are fishing for me,
All the big house are in love with my money, save only he.

I'm frank with you—that is my way; but really I
 like you, though
You neither like me nor trust me, as well by your
 looks I know;
And now you are wondering why I am set on this
 weak-witted earl :—
As if strong-witted peers would look at a mere
 Colonial girl.

Now, I've told you the truth, will you help me?
 These women will drive him mad;
Their nagging and sneering and mocking have
 broken what spirit he had.
Folk talk of the fourth generation, that it would
 bring back their wit—
I'm not superstitious, mind ye—but what if there's
 something in it?

Most of the old stock here are needing fresh blood
 in their veins,
And I'm sane enough to set up a score of their
 weak scatter-brains;
What say you?—might I not risk it just on the
 chance that they
Might get a new start in life to go on in a rational
 way?

You smile—it's a dubious smile, I've noticed it often
    on you—
Oh you do not trust me, I know, yet you might, if
    you only knew;
No matter; you'll take me with you? I'll not spoil
    sport if I can,
I just want a lesson from you how to manage a
    moody young man."

So we went off on our fishing, but our sport was
    little that day;
He was not once at his ease, and I saw that he
    wished her away;
Nor did she manage him wisely, she had not the
    delicate touch,
As she chattered and laughed on briskly, to know
    when it was too much.

Yet she meant well, I am certain; meant landing
    her fish, if she could,
But yet to make life to him brighter, and banish
    his gloomy mood;
And she bit her thin lip at the failure, when he
    went off in a dream;
That was the last time that ever he threw a gut-
    line on the stream.

How it came round then, I know not; they wanted to wipe off the debt,
And she with her millions of dollars would buy her an old coronet;
They settled it somehow among them, and got him to church one day,
Where he stood like a man in a trance, but he said what he had to say.

The young folk travelled abroad for a time, as their way is, you know;
And the Dowager followed with Ion too, after a month or so,
We heard of them sometimes in Paris, and then in Rome for a while,
And by and by on the Rhine river, then off for a trip to the Nile.

At last, they came home, and were followed by visitors, Princes and Dukes,
And priests with the subtlest smiles, and the sleekest of sidelong looks,
Black-bearded foreign nobles and their beardless foreign priests,
And oh but there were rare doings with hunts and balls and feasts.

You see, if there was not an heir—as there did
    not seem like to be—
Our young lady, she would be countess; and now
    there was money to free
Every acre of debt, and to leave the Australian
    girl
Enough to maintain the state of the widow of Fing-
    land's Earl.

That was a merry time then; they rode to the hunt
    by day,
And kept up the ball till morning, or shuffled the
    cards for play,
All but the Earl, and he went moping and mooning
    about,
Alone in his dusky chamber, or alone in the woods
    without.

The young wife did as the rest, she rode to the
    meet, at least,
Saw them throw off, and then came ambling home
    with a priest,
Chatted and laughed in the parlour, sailed through
    a waltz at the ball,
And, thinking nothing of Ughtred, made herself
    pleasant to all.

So it went on, till a day when bills must be settled
    at last;
They had been falling like snow-flakes white on the
    old house cast,
And duns had been prowling about it, threatening
    letters been sent;
What could it mean, these people growing so
    insolent?

Where was the chamberlain? Why had those men
    never been paid?
Where were the millions of dollars for which they
    had boldly played?
What had "my Lady" to do with it? was not her
    money my Lord's?
Had she not titles and honours for her squatter
    father's hoards?

Then they learnt what it meant, that glitter of steel
    in her eye;
Surely poor folk must be paid for the things that
    the rich folk buy,
And her lady mother and Ion had ordered every
    thing nice,
And, of course, she had always supposed they were
    careful to count the price.

G

As for her money—her father who honestly had come by it,
Had tied it up, every penny, as fast as the law could tie it;
Her marriage was not a joint-stock; each managed their own affairs;
Not a dollar of hers was Ughtred's, and never a penny was theirs.

Ay! they had met their match; it was even so as she said;
The lawyers had warned the Earl; but he never was strong in the head,
Folk even doubted, at times, if he knew what his marriage meant,
And as for the signing of papers—he had signed whatever was sent.

So she sat smiling there calmly, and spoke in the blandest way
Soft lisping words that were daggers; how could she know but that they—
She was but a squatter's daughter—had only to clap their hands,
And slaves would bring dresses and jewels, and horses and houses and lands?

But, of course, if their money was gone they must
    live in a quieter way;
No ladies, as she supposed, would wear what they
    could not pay;
And she knew that one could be happy, as free
    from the burden of cares,
In a hut with a maid-of-all-work as in a great
    castle like theirs.

Oh the glitter of that blue eye! yet it showed too
    a gleam of fun,
As she told them of mutton and damper and tea
    on her father's "run,"
Cooked by herself, with a wild Irish girl who saw
    to the fire;—
It was spiteful, no doubt; but the sketch was
    cleverly hit off by her.

What could they do? They might rage, but she
    shrugged her shoulders, and smiled;
If they could not pay their own tradesmen, why,
    then she had been beguiled;
She had known that he was not burdened with
    brains, nor in vigorous health,
But she took all their stories for gospel, when they
    spoke of his greatness and wealth.

So the ladies and princes and dukes and priests all
    vanished like smoke,
And our clever Colonial countess had all her own
    way with the folk,
And we soon had an orderly household and thrifty,
    yet stately withal,
And just a year after the wedding there came a
    young heir to it all.

I think she had honestly tried to help the poor
    Earl in his fits
And moods, till it plainly appeared he was fairly
    out of his wits,
Harmless enough, but nothing was left of his brains
    but the husk,
And he muttered a deal to himself as he wandered
    about in the dusk.

I had not seen him for years, till I met him this
    evening by chance,
In the wood, and as soon as he saw me, he looked
    with a furtive glance
This side and that, like a wild beast, to find what
    way he could go,
For we were on the narrow path 'tween the rock
    and the river below.

So he turned right round, and made for the beech-
 wood, sir; but my stride
Is longer than his, and soon I was walking along
 by his side;
I hoped that my good Lord was well; and his folk
 would be glad to see
More of him now and then: and did he remember
 me?

We used to go fishing together; and would he not
 like now to try—
The stream was in beautiful trim—to cast a line and
 a fly!
"I seem to have seen you before," he knitted his
 brows, and said,
As if he were catching at something; "My friend,
 have you long been dead?

Why are you all so restless? this place now is
 haunted with ghosts;
They come out singly by day, but at night they are
 trooping in hosts;
No one sees them, but I; it's the second sight, you
 know,
Sir Lachlan brought when he married the heiress
 long ago."

Poor fellow! He had been fumbling a while
    with his seals and chain,
Still looking this side and that for a way of escape,
    but in vain,
Till now when he suddenly plunged down into a
    deep-sunk dell
Strewn with brachen and moss where the shy deer
    love to dwell.

I saw them leaping up near, and laying their horns
    on their back
As they sought for a lonelier dingle, while he went
    on in their track,
And there was a lump in my throat, sir, as I sat
    me down on a stone
And heard him mutter and stumble and still keep
    hurrying on.

Think of it, sir; when you climb there up to the
    top of the Ben,
Up through the oak and the pine wood, and the
    birch and juniper then,
Up through the belt of heather, and past where the
    moss only grows,
Till you reach the bare scalp of the rock with its
    lichens and rifted snows;

And there as you stand, at last, looking north and south and west,
Far as the eye can see from the crag of the eagle's nest,
Cornland, woodland, moorland, every acre is his
And the villages down on the beach where the wild wan water is:

And there are three old burghs too, paying him stents and dues,
With hamlets maybe a score, and farms and crofts and feus,
And over the highland border there are miles of moor and moss,
You cannot see from the Ben, where the deer their antlers toss.

And yonder he is, poor fellow, wandering by night in the dew,
Hurrying by day through the thickest shades of the pine and yew;
It's Nebuchadnezzar once more summering, wintering out
Among the black horned cattle, or where the screech owls shout.

What a heritage that, sir! a cup filled up to the brim,
Yet never a drop can he taste, and it stands there mocking at him!
There is my boy now, barefoot, paddling about in the stream,
His life is a fact at least, but the Earl's—it is only a dream.

What can you make of it, sir? Is it Fate, as the people aver?
Our Lady is shrewd, and they tell me the young Lord takes after her,
Is more of the squatter kind than the noble of high degree,
But good at his books, and his manners, like her's, are frank and free.

I have not much faith in weirds, though the Lord's Law says, it is true,
The third and fourth generation may reap the wrong that you do;
Yet God does not do much cursing, nor tie it in long entails,
Not in the female line, but still to be heired by the males.

And I have some faith in Love, that it might have brought all right,
As sunshine quickens the seed with its play of warmth and light;
Yet he never got much of that, sir, from sister, mother or wife,
And I cannot get over the thought, that they wasted a gentle life.

Never a pleasanter lad, sir,—nothing was wrong with him then—
Cast e'er a line on the river, or stalked the red deer in the glen;
But they must thwart his first love, and none to give him had they—
And then forsooth it was heaven had taken his reason away.

Ay, ay! God and heaven, it's little we heed their say,
When good might come of our keeping the straight and narrow way,
But they're handy to lay the blame on, when things go wrong at last,
And you need a glisk of religion to glamour the days that are past.

Provost Chivas.

Come, Martin, don't stand stiffly there;
Be seated now, and draw the chair
    A little closer to the fire;
It's winter weather, see, without;
And I would talk with you about
    Old days, before our day expire.

NOTE.—The story of Peter Williamson revealed, in the last century, a strange tale of the kidnapping of boys in our towns by the magistrates and leading citizens, and sending them to the Plantations virtually as slaves. That is the origin of this poem.

What will you take, now? Nothing! nay,
I know what you're about to say;
   You know your place: but that is pride—
You think you are quite as good as I;
And so you are; there, don't be shy:
   Your place is here, man, at my side.

Look, Martin; we are growing old:
Why should you be so stiff and cold,
   And look as if you hated all—
The wine, the table, and the seat,
The Turkey carpet 'neath your feet,
   The very pictures on the wall?

I stopt you on the high street once,
But you—you gave me not a chance
   To tell you what was in my heart;
Though I was Provost at the time,
You looked at me as if a crime
   Might bring me soon to the hangman's cart.

And Bailie Webbe was at my side,
And vowed for such contempt and pride
   He would have had you in the dock;

Of course, I did not dream of that,
But yet you might have raised your hat,
   And done for once like other folk.

Nay, Martin, do not turn away;
Our day is short, our hairs are grey,
   It's time to grease our boots for going;
Why should we fall out, when we meet,
Like strange dogs snarling on the street?
   We have small space for quarrels growing.

I mind me, we were boys together;
In summer's sun and winter weather
   We padded, barefoot, to the school;
Boys were not nice and dainty then
With shoes and hats like little men;
   They bred us on the Spartan rule.

As lads too we were seldom parted,
True friends and loving and one-hearted,
   Though now and then we had our jars:
Each night I would convoy you home,
Then back with me you needs must come,
   Talking of poetry and the stars,

Or of the sermon we had heard
On Sabbath from the Holy Word,
  Or of the minister, good and true,
Who christened us, and made us sit
Together, when the time was fit,
  Down at the holy table too.

Ay, ay! it's good to think of these
Good days and high solemnities,
  That linked us close when we were youths:
Why should we not have many a walk
Together still, and cheerful talk
  About these everlasting truths?

Well, yes; I grant the blame was mine
At first, yet lately it was thine
  Who would not help to heal the breach:
And, man, it does not mend one's song
To know that one was in the wrong,
  When friends went drifting out of reach.

It could not well be helped, besides;
This man must walk, while that one rides:
  And even the holy prophet says

That in this race of life, of course,
The footman runs not with the horse,
   And so we took our several ways;

And I grew rich, and you were poor;
Yet you've the best of it, I'm sure,
   My money, man, it's like a curse:
I wish you had it—no, I don't;
For sure there is no blessing on't,
   And it would only make you worse.

Yes, Martin, houses, lands and gold
Bring little comfort when you're old,
   Or honours which the world can give:
But you've had love to sweeten life,
A happy home, and faithful wife,
   Though that wild laddie made her grieve.

Now, do not sniff and sneer at me;
Folk call me Lord by courtesy,
   But not in scorn, nor yet in sport;
Remember I've been Provost twice,
And given the government advice,
   And was presented too at Court.

You should respect my office, even
If to the man may not be given
   The honour which he thinks his due;—
And for your son, no doubt, it's sad,
Although he was a worthless lad,
   If all accounts of him be true.

They say he broke his mother's heart;
They say that he was art and part
   With them that robbed the County Bank
Well, well; it's natural for you
To say that's false; they say it's true;
   And sure enough he swore and drank.

Only a thoughtless boy!—more shame
To bring dishonour on your name,
   And vex a mother fond and true!
And she was all that, I am told—
Indeed, I know—as good as gold;
   And such a comely woman too!

Ah! Martin, you were fortunate
To find so excellent a mate;
   Though she is gone now, is she not?

Gone to a better, happier land—
Give me a grip, man, of your hand;
   But death is our appointed lot.

Ay, ay! this world is full of change;
A tangled hank it is, and strange
   With ups and downs, and loss and gain,
And here to-day, and there to-morrow,
And nothing certain here but sorrow:—
   Enough to puzzle heart and brain.

Nay, nay; don't go yet, Martin, stay;
You've heard about your son, you say?
   I'm glad of it for your sake, man:
But for this trumped-up story now,
It's quite absurd, you must allow,
   And you must stop him, for you can.

He'll get into worse trouble yet
Unless he hold his peace on it,
   I warn you fairly while it's time;
They say that from his earliest youth
He ne'er was known to speak the truth,
   And was convicted once of crime.

That may be false, or may be true ;
But, Martin, I appeal to you :
   You are a man of sense : just think !
To charge those men who represent
Order and law and government,
   That they at any crime could wink !

The provost, bailies, city clerk,
The men of highest rank and mark,
   The rulers of your native town,
And men of quality, beside,
Who shall be nameless, but are tried
   And faithful servants of the crown,

Was ever Judge or jury yet
Could be persuaded these had set
   Common and Statute law at nought?
They're liker, man, to hold that he
Is guilty of Lese-majesty—
   And that's a grave crime even in thought.

It's true there were some gutter boys—
Rogues, always bent on thievish ploys—
   Who, for the town's good and their own

Were 'prenticed to some honest men
In the plantations, now and then—
   Good riddance too as can be shewn.

And if you'll read them I will lend
The grateful letters that they send
   About their happy life abroad,
With plenty wage, and plenty food,
And pious ministers and good
   Who guide them on the better road.

'Twould do your heart, man, good to read
What wholesome, useful lives they lead,
   Instead of prowling in the street,
Now begging bits, now stealing bits,
And living badly on their wits,
   With ill-clad backs and ill-shod feet.

And for the Indians, now, they say
These hardly ever come their way,
   And when they do, it is to truck
Powder and guns for beavers' skins,
And drops of drink for moccasins,
   Or horns of buffalo or buck.

A better country theirs than ours
Where cadgers claim their rights and powers,
   And tinkers will have law on you!
I sometimes wish that I were there,
Free from the burden and the care
   Of thankless work I have to do.

But for your son, you'll stop his plea;
Of course, it's nothing, man, to me
   Although it's hard, when one is old,
To have been Provost once, and then
Be charged with stealing boys and men,
   And selling them for lust of gold.

I'm glad for your sake that the lad
Turns up again, though he was bad
   Before, and seems no better now;
But if he will persist to blame
His betters, there's against his name
   Enough to hang him yet, I trow.

Just tell him if he'll hold his peace,
And bid that lawyer's "clavers" cease,
   Who says whate'er he's paid to say,

The town wants some one to engage
For little work and plenty wage,
   And I might put it in his way.

A bribe! no, no; it is not fit
That you should look that way at it;
   Martin, you pull me up too short:
I only meant, if he should want
A job of work—and work is scant—
   It's well to have a friend at Court.

And he must choose between this chance
And being led a bonny dance,
   Through courts of Law, for crimes and debts,—
Hame-sucken, stouthrief, common theft,
Smuggling, and heavy claims he left
   For gambling and horse-racing bets.

Or man or boy, it matters not;
These pleas against him will be brought,
   And there's a long purse too behind;
Think ye that Provost, Bailies, Clerk
Will let a messan-dog come bark
   Right at their heels, and never mind?

It is not reason, man: be sure
They'll play their game, and find a cure
   For their hurt honour at any cost;
They'll plea it in the inner court,
They'll plea it to the last resort
   Before they let the game be lost.

Law is the hardest mill to grind,
Nor is it water, man, or wind,
   But gold that makes its wheels to go,
And ere the Inner House we're through,
I doubt it will be hard for you
   A plack or penny more to show.

But you can stop it if you will;
And maybe manage even to fill
   The purse which it would empty soon:
Now, do not play the fool, and rob
Your age for such an idle job,
   Which is like reaching for the moon.

I do not say the thing was right
Exactly, now I have more light,
   Though no one blamed it at the time;

The very ministers would say,
Each time the laddies went away,
　　It saved them from a life of crime.

We gave them clothes, we gave them meat,
And shoes and stockings for their feet,
　　Which seldom they had known before:
We saw too their indentures writ,
And signed and sealed as sure as wit
　　Of man could do. What could we more?

And when the ship would sail away,
We had a minister to pray
　　With the poor laddies, as was right.
And, oh how earnest they would plead
That waifs and prodigals, the seed
　　Of righteous men, might yet get light!

And now to charge us with offence,
Because we made, perhaps, some pence—
　　It was a trifle at the most—
Clearing our streets of rogues and thieves
Who grew there thick as Autumn leaves
　　That from November woods are tossed!

Think, Martin; to be charged with crime,
I who have lived here all my time,
   Respected in my native town!
And, maybe, see my little gear,
Gathered through many a busy year,
   Escheated some day to the Crown!

That's hard, you surely must allow:
And all for what? Just tell me how
   Was I to know these Chippeways—
Incarnate fiends!—would hack and hew,
And burn and torture, as they do:
   That is, if all is true he says.

Nay, Martin, do not look like that,
And knit your brows, and grip your hat;
   Well; yes, it's true that I did make
Some statement once about your child—
For I with rage and fear was wild—
   And maybe it was a mistake.

I wronged him? yes; he may have been
All that you say; for I am clean
   Distraught and maddened now about

This business; will you not have pity?
'Twill bring shame on your native city:
   And you could easily pull us out.

Give me some drink, then, if you'll not
Take it yourself: it's some I got
   To toast our friendship once again;
But that, it seems, is not to be—
My hand is shaking: let me see,
   What was I saying?—Yes, it's plain:

You mean to plead this case, and I
Will fight it till the day I die
   Through Outer House, and Inner House,
And House of Lords, though there should be
No more of all my property
   Than might give house-room to a mouse.

It's war—and all is fair in war:
Things can't be worse than now they are;
   And you and your's what should I heed?
I'm to be once more Provost soon,
And we'll all sing the self-same tune,
   For all the Council are agreed.

We will not brook this scaith and shame,
We will not lose our own good name
  For vagabonds and gutter bairns
The town is better far without;
And he is like the rest, no doubt,
  Of no more use than brachen-ferns.

Ay! leave me now: I tell you true,
It shames me to have bowed to you,
  A fellow poor as any rat,
Who thinks to fight the Clerk and me,
The Bailies, too, and Quality
  With such a trumpery tale as that!

I thought at first you had some heart,
Some sense, at least to play the part
  Which any man of judgment would:
But there: I'm done with you: away!
You'd better make friends while you may,
  You'll need them, for our names are good.

There's Little-mills and Chokit-burn,
Woodside and Tarvet, Drums and Durn
  And Bees-wood too and Otterslack,

PROVOST CHIVAS.

And Bailie Webbe, and Bailie Sym,
And the Town Clerk—take note of him—
   He has the bank, too, at his back.

And you would mell with all of these!
Man, saw ye ever a skep of bees
   O'erturned, and how they buzz and sting:
I pity you, with such a crew
Upon you, and the lawyers too,
   And all the heavy costs they bring.

Take thought, e'en, yet while it is time:
It's a grave thing to charge a crime
   On honest men and Magistrates:
Better your son had never come
Than bring such ruin on your home,
   And also waste our braw estates.

Remember all our early days,
Remember all our kindly ways,
   Remember that bit post of profit,
With little work and plenty wage:
I think I almost might engage
   That you should have refusal of it.

You will not?   Nay, then, off with you !
And do the worst that you can do ;
   I've been too humble to you, sir.

(*Solus.*)

Woe's me ! the house and land and gear,
And Provost's chain and badge next year !
   And oh, 'twill make an awful stir !

And though we'll brave it out, I doubt
   The thing will hardly bear inspection ;
These lawyers' tongues will fleer and flout,
The Judge too will have turn about
   In that unsparing vivisection.

And lose or win, we'll have to pay ;
   A lawyer's tongue's a costly dish :—
Better the ship had sailed away
To Newfoundland or Hudson's Bay,
   Or north for Greenland's whales to fish.

I wish the job were now to do ;
   I would not be so rash or fain :
Yet we had merry evenings too,
When each his share of profits drew,
   And counted up his honest gain.

Good were the suppers, and the wine
    Was mellow at the Lemon Tree,
And cheery was our talk, and fine
The wit which never crossed the line
    Proper to men of our degree.

Pity our merry nights should bring
    Bad mornings, as they mostly do!
Why should the honey have a sting?
Why should this fellow come to wring
    Good money from our purses too?

It's very hard that Providence
    Can never leave our minds at ease;
For me, I cannot see the sense
Of raking up an old offence
    To waste our means on Lawyer's fees.

Morgana.

Oh, green are the pines of the Barleywood,
　And the drooping birches are fair to see,
And bonnie the carpet that summer weaves
Of the green overlapping brachen leaves;
　And the spring blue-bell and anemone
　　You might bind up there in sheaves.

And blythe are the birds in the Barleywood,
　Where merle and mavis and woodlark sing,
And the cushat croodles high unseen,
And the cuckoo calls from the brachen green;
　And sweet are the smells that the wind-wafts
　　　bring,
　　When the morning airs are keen.

But woe is me for the Barleywood!
  There's a pang in my heart for every tree,
And for every bird in the wood that dwells,
And for every waft of the woodland smells;
    The pang of a cruel memory
      For all its buds and bells.

For fairest things may dreariest be,
  And sweetest of songs most sad to hear,
When tree and blossom and bird and flower
All link them on to a woful hour,
  And bring the past and its sorrow near,
    The heart to overpower.

There were two lovers that sought my love—
  Ay me! but it's ever so long ago—
One was beautiful, young and brave,
But the other was noble and rich and grave:
  And how should a silly young maiden know
    Fittingly to behave?

I had no mother to guide me right—
  Ah, woe! for a thoughtless girl like me!
And my father he left me all the day,
And went to his sleep in the evening grey;
  And how should a foolish maiden see
    Rightly to guide her way?

I loved my beautiful youth and brave—
    Lack-a-day! I was still in my teens—
Yet I longed for the wealth and the noble name,
But I had not a thought of sin or shame;
    And how should a girl know what it means
        To keep from evil fame?

My Lord, he came, when the day was high—
    And oh but the hours went heavy and slow—
But my Love stole quietly up to my side,
And low at my feet in the evening sighed,
    And then would the hours like minutes flow
        In the happy eventide.

My Lord, he would hold my worsted hank,
    Pleased when my needle was briskly plied;
But my Love would not hear of work to do
When he was with me, and well he knew
    To make the happy hours swiftly glide
        With love that was always new.

And close to his heart he clasped me once—
    Oh what so sweet as a love-embrace?
My Lord, he would only touch the tip
Of my little hand with a dainty lip,
    And then smile prettily into my face
        And let the little hand slip.

But my love he clasped me once and twice—
   How I thrilled all through in his fond embrace!
And he vowed, if ever my Lord should dare
To hold me so, that he did not care
   What might happen of foul disgrace,
     He would not leave me there.

I wist not then what his words might mean,
   But oh his look it was fierce and wild,
It frightened me so, that I bade him go:
And my Lord he spake to me sweet and low,
   Next day and next, and I heard and smiled,
     And did not say him No.

But by and by a low whisper ran—
   It should have blistered every tongue—
Ran through the evil-speaking place,
Whisper wicked of foul disgrace:
   And I so simple and pure and young!
     Oh it was vile and base.

He was a villain, I said, and lied—
   Ah me! what can a poor girl do?—
He lied, he lied: I had nothing to hide;
Yet, he struck me down when I was a bride,
   Pierced my heart with a falsehood through:
     Oh how the villain lied!

My Lord, he came of a noble race,
    And yes! his heart it was noble too;
Lo! now, he said, this lie has gone
All through the city, and there are none,
    But only I, that believe in you,
        And still keep loving on.

But I have trusted you, and I trust—
    I took his hand, and I kissed it then—
Yes, I trust, for I know you true,
And I should die if I doubted you;
    And I scorn the women and viler men
        Who lie now as they do.

Then let the wedding bells ring out,
    And let the priest make haste and come;
Our name was ever without a stain,
And they will tattle and talk in vain,
    When we to the altar go, and home
        Return together again.

It was a hard and a cruel place,
    Where every man of his neighbour spoke,
And evil report of sin or wrong
Grew louder still as it went along,
    Till on some happy life it broke
        And silenced its happy song.

Had I only thought! But my heart was hot;
   I am certain now that he was belied,
For there were women that hated me
Because men said I was fair to see;
    And women will humble woman's pride,
      False as the tale may be.

But I was mad: and I said, he lies;
   Oh is there none who will take my part?
Were I a man, I would lay him low,
And who shall give him a right death blow,
    Him I will love with all my heart
      For slaying the villain so.

Slowly, slowly my Lord he rose—
   And oh but he looked grave and sad:
And he bent him low, and he went his way,
Never a word then did he say,
    And my heart leaped up, and I was glad,
      Until the close of day.

But all that night I found no sleep,
   Tossing in restless, troubled thought;
I said I would love my Lord truly and well,
I said I was happy, and yet there fell
    Such gloom on my heavy heart as brought
      Horror on me like hell.

All through the night I lay, and tossed,
  Wearily longing for the day,
And rose at dawn in a troubled mood,
And hied me away to the Barley-wood,
    And through its dewy glades took my way,
    Where the air was fresh and good.

Sweet smelled the pines of the Barley-wood,
  And oh I shall never forget the birds,
They gathered about me, and had no fear,
And sang the thought of my heart as clear
    As if they were speaking it out in words --
    His lie shall cost him dear!

And I too sang, yet I was not glad;
  I said I was, but it was not so:
I sang as the mad folk I have known
Sing, when their heart is like a stone,
    But I could have wept with joy to know
    No fell deed had been done.

Just then, and ever so near, I heard—
  Ah me! how they ring in my heart this day!
Two shots, and a thud on the dewy grass—
O heart! my heart, how it sunk alas!
    Oh cruel madness, and evil day
    That brought this thing to pass!

Well did I know what had befallen,—
  As well as if I had seen it all—
Great Lords have a steady hand and eye,
They sleep, and they do not fear to die:
    But my young Love for sleep would call,
    And it would not come nigh.

Well did I wot what had befallen,—
  As well as if I had seen it all—
And out of the wood I rushed, and there
My Love lay dead in the morning air,
    Close by the mossy brambly wall,
    Upon the moorland bare.

I fell on him, and I clasped him close—
  Oh how the love of him all came back!
Men were near me, standing about,
But I only saw the blood oozing out
    From his dear mouth in a thread-like track,
    That killed all hope and doubt.

Beautiful there in death he lay,
  But ah the cold damp on his brow!
Oh my beautiful, young, and brave!
I—it is I that have dug your grave!
    And oh that I were but with you now!
    For Death is the boon I crave.

I kissed his mouth—I kissed his cheek—
 O Love, my love! I wildly cried:
The red blood stained my mouth and chin,
And the stain of it was on my soul within;
 For I was his murderer: yes, he lied:
  But oh my sin, my sin!

It was in the madness of Love he lied:
 And I—I loved him in spite of it:
Come back, my Love: come back, my Life:
Will none of you thrust in my heart a knife?
 For I surely might overtake him yet,
  And be his own true wife.

He lied, but I would have done it too,
 Had he been false to his love and me;
Leave us here: how I hate you now;
There's a lock of fair hair on his brow—
 I have curled it oft on my finger; see
  It knows my finger now:

Oh I would not give that lock of hair
 For all your lordship and your land:
But bury us both together here;
And come not hither to drop a tear,
 You who slew him with your hand,
  And me with the murderous cheer.

Mad I was and unjust to him—
  What would you have from a breaking heart?
He was too noble to take it ill;
Besides, they hurried him down the hill,
  And far away to a foreign part
    Where he is wandering still.

They made a bier of the green pine-boughs—
  Ay me! the Barley-wood pines are sweet!
A bier for him and a bier for me,
For I was as like to death as he,
  And they bore us down to my Father's seat,
    A woeful sight to see.

Yet I lived on, who would have gone
  So glad with my love to his early rest;
My hair grew white, but not with years,
And I lived down all their lies and sneers,
  But with a heavy heart in my breast,
    And many sighs and tears.

Never I saw my Lord again,
  Never I wished to see his face;
Yet he was sure of a noble strain,
Trusty and true; but it would be pain
  Recalling the tale of foul disgrace,
    And all that past again.

One thing only has made me glad—
After the healing mercy of God—
The day of the Duel now is past;
And never shall maiden stare aghast,
   As I did then, on the blood-tinged sod
   Where my dead Love was cast.

Mrs. Coventry.

Wh'sht! John; why should you aye complain
    Of trade and profits being bad,
And cry about your little gain,
    And moan at every loss you've had?
You have more money than you know
    What to do with, man. God has blessed
Your labour, and you ought to show
    His bounty has not been misplaced.

Sometimes I almost pity Him,
    Sometimes I'm clean ashamed to pray,
Seeing our cup filled to the brim,
    And so much goodness thrown away!

It must be hard to bear, I think,
   To be replenishing folk's store
With wealth of clothes and meat and drink,
   And hear them crying still for more.

It's easier learning how to win,
   Than how to use wealth as we should:
And though we gain it without sin,
   It's sin to have, and do no good
With what we have; and what is worse,
   It eats the heart like rust or rot:
Think, now, if there should be a curse
   Wrapt up in every hoarded note.

When we were young, John, we were poor,
   And yet we were far richer then;
We sent no beggar from the door,
   Nor grudged the wage of working men:
We had enough, and some to spare
   For them that were worse off than we;
And there was sunshine in the air
   Each night when you came home to me.

But now the pocket's buttoned up,
   The beggar comes not to our door,
He knows there's neither bite nor sup
   For tramps, as used to be before:

Ah well! maybe they're mostly rogues:
　　There were rogues too when we were young,
Yet none were driven away like dogs;
　　And even tramps' hearts may be wrung.

There's none will speak to you as I
　　Am free to do, who love you best:
I dare not flatter you, and lie
　　With a false heart upon your breast.
And, O John, but your wealth has made
　　A hard bit on that breast for me,
That does not give an easy head,
　　And is not as it used to be.

O ay! you give me all I need,
　　And more than all I care to get
For gowns and gawds, and meat to feed
　　Us all, and ne'er to be in debt;
There's plenty on ourselves to spend,
　　E'en more, I think, than's good for health;
But, think ye, was that God's chief end
　　In giving you that heap of wealth?

I've heard you say it's hard to find
　　Investments safe—and thought that odd:
But here is one just to your mind,
　　A good investment, John, with God:

They never lose who lend to Him,
   They get good interest, indeed;
And that poor man who broke his limb,
   Has five wee helpless bairns to feed.

Nay, do not grudge it, man: God loves
   A cheerful giver: e'en be glad
That you can help the bonnie doves
   Left hungry there at home and sad—
There; take it back; I want to get
   A blessing for you, John, from heaven;
But they who grudge to pay their debt
   To God, shall find no blessing given.

We have no bairns at our fireside;
   God would not send His children here
To folk whose hearts are full of pride,
   And set on hoarding worldly gear.
They'd only learn, what makes them worse,
   To hanker for the gold they see:—
No; this is not a house to nurse
   God's little ones, as they should be.

And who's to heir it all, since we
   Are childless? Is it not a sin
To leave a fruitful legacy
   Of quarrels to the next of kin,

When we could gladden many a home,
    And brighten many a sunless life,
And lift up for the days to come,
    Maybe, some hapless child or wife?

How freely, John, we used to give
    To every holy cause and good,
When it was hard enough to live,
    For then you would do as you should;
The Kirk was never then forgot,
    You never did neglect the poor,
You pitied too the sick man's lot,
    And sought his comfort and his cure.

Yet then your mite was more to you
    Than is your five-pound note to-day,
For there was something you must do
    Without, to give the mite away;
You wore the old coat for a time,
    That some one might get warmth from you;
And I—I thought the old coat sublime,
    Because the heart beneath was true.

O John, this big house, and the host
    Of lazy servants, full of meat,
And carriages and horses cost
    The poor what they have need to eat:

And cost you too; you used to speak
  Of books, and made me blythe and gay,
But now it's funds through all the week,
  And markets even on Sabbath day.

And you must buy a fine estate,
  And shoot your rabbits and your hares,
And dine and visit with the great,
  And sometimes even put on their airs,
And send your poachers to the gaol,
  And set your keepers o'er the fish:
O man, can you forget how well
  Ye liked to catch a dainty dish?

That's a braw greenhouse; and it's true
  I like the bonnie flowers; but yet
You made me happier, John, when you
  Brought me the box of mignonette.
The greenhouse speaks to me of gold,
  And it may bide, or may depart;
But still I keep the box that told
  About the kind and thoughtful heart.

O man, let 'Change and Market be!
  Let others get their turn; and come,
Just think how pleasant it would be
  To have once more the old sweet home,

To read together in the mirk,
　Together mercy to invoke,
To walk together to the Kirk,
　And do some good to other folk.

I'm weary of this grand display,
　And hearing of the rise and fall
Of prices; would I were away
　From ships and yarns and funds and all:
Oh if the Lord would only take,
　And lift our hearts to things above!
Or else some bank, perhaps, would break
　And leave us nought but health and love?

Mother and Step-Mother.

Oh my baby, my sweet, my Own!
   Oh, joy to have one to love like this!
And love like this to be so bestown!
   Oh, the wonder of it, and bliss!
Look at me, baby, with those deep eyes,
   Smile to me, baby, with those soft lips!
Oh, the tremulous thrills that rise
   At the fine touch of those finger tips!

And yet you fill me with fear and awe,
   God's little child, that He gave to me
To rear you up in His Love and Law,
   For the life that is, and that is to be;

Lo! Heaven is looking out from the blue
　　And solemn depths of those great eyes;
How shall I keep you pure and true?
　　How shall I make you just and wise?

I promised to mother those babes of his,
　　And, oh, I have tried to pay my vow;
But I did not know what a mother is,
　　I did not know, as I know it now.
I loved them for his sake, and always will;
　　Poor motherless babes, I love them yet;
But motherless babes they must be still,
　　For I cannot love them like you, my pet.

They're very nice, and they've been so good.
　　And they really are fond of me, as they say;
But they're not like my blossom of ladyhood,
　　And they have not their father's gentle way.
No doubt, they take after the mother, and she
　　Was vulgar—her picture shows that right;
And there's something in them—it is plain to see
　　They never will grow to be ladies quite.

Well, yes; she was pretty, and so are they;
　　She has sandy curls, and she wears a wreath,
And her eyes are meaningless cold and grey,
　　And her lips are parted to shew her teeth.

She has dumpy hands, but she thinks them fine—
   It's all in her picture, baby dear—
And the painter has hinted a sullen line
   Across her brow, with a shade of fear.

I often look at that picture now
   Which hangs in the nursery as it should,
And I watch for the faint line on the brow
   When her children are ever in angry mood:
I never have seen it, I'm bound to say,
   Though it may come yet, as they grow old;
Still I never have seen it, and never may,—
   Yet these things run in the blood, I'm told.

He does not speak of her much to me,
   Though he does to his children, which is right;
I tell him to do it, and sometimes he
   Sits by their beds, and talks at night.
For, oh, were I taken, my pet, from you,
   I should like you to hear of me from your
      father:—
Should I like him to give you a step-mother too?
   Nay, let us die together rather.

I talk to you, baby, as I can
   Unto no other but you, my pet:

There's a nook in my heart which my own good
  man—
 And he's very good—has not been in yet:
It is there where I think of his former wife,
 And the picture up in the nursery,
And wonder if they had peace or strife,
 And if he could love her as he loves me

Oh, baby, it's hard to fill my post?
 But yes! I will love her children more;
They shall not feel that for you they lost
 One touch of the love that they had before.
I cannot give them my own baby's part,
 That's yours, my darling, whatever befall;
But, oh, your coming has filled my heart
 More and more with the love of all.

Bailie Butters and Young Dinwoodie.

Two men in a cosy Hostel sitting
   By a sea-coal fire, in a cheerful light,
While past the window were shadows flitting
   Through the fog of a dull November night,
Were cracking their walnuts after dinner,
   With dry-palate olives to flavour the wine,
Hardly feeling like saint or sinner,
   But that it was good for a man to dine.

One was a smooth, smug, florid, pot-bellied
   Clean-shaven man, of a portly mould,
With tremulous cheeks, as if nicely jellied,
   And coloured with port-wine rich and old;

The other an Exquisite, long-limbed, sprawling
  Low on an easy soft-cushioned seat,
Lisping his words, and slowly drawling
  Thoughts that ran on at a fever-heat.

Quoth the pot-bellied one : " You were saying
  Life's not worth living; you're wrong, sir, quite :
This world, though it's not just for idling and playing,
  Is the best of all worlds if you take it right.
It is not the heaven folk see before 'em,
  When they fall in love at a country dance,
But I've seen more than you of its *variorum*,
  And I'd live it again, if I had the chance.

Not worth living, sir! If you are sober,
  Honest and willing to do its work,
Hating a rogue and a thief and a robber,
  And playing a fairly good knife and fork—
For I admit that if one is dyspeptic
  He cannot well live as a good man should :
His bad digestion will make him skeptic
  Of all that is happy and right and good—

But let him be sober and prudent and willing
  To work, as he should, till his sixty years,
With his wits about him to turn a shilling,
  And know a good thing, when his chance appears,

Let him be civil, and follow the leading
   Of common sense just, whatever he's at,
And his life shall be pleasant as novel-reading—
   And I am myself now a proof of that.

I was poor enough when I was a lad, sir;
   Hadn't a copper for some folk's pound;
Yet most of them, by and by, went to the bad, sir,
   And God knows where they are now to be found;
But I worked at anything that was going,
   And I saved up every penny I could;
And my ventures grew as my cash was growing,
   And whatever I promised, my word was good:

Yes! I was poor, when first I started,
   And should have been poor still, according to you,
If God does not care though we're all broken-hearted,
   But just goes His own way whatever we do;
Yet here I am, sir; I'm nobody's debtor,
   And I lay a calm head on my pillow at night,
For God has been good—He could scarce have been better—
   To order things rightly, because I did right.

Now if I had taken to gambling and drinking,
   Do you think I should be where I am to-day

With funds in the Bank and the Stocks—though
  they're sinking
Almost a quarter, I'm sorry to say?—
Never, sir. But there's a God up in heaven
  Who always takes care of respectable folk;
And what better proof of it could there be given?—
  I feel that my faith is placed firm on a rock.

I had not a shilling once; but I determined
  That I would take warning by what I had seen;
And look to me now: not a judge ever ermined
  Drinks better port wine, with a conscience more
    clean;
My wife is a model; my children are pictures;
  My business is thriving; my home, come and see
How its happiness wholly refutes all your strictures,
  And tells a plain tale for my Maker and me.

Oh I'm grateful to Him! Yes; of course, I've had
    losses;
  There is no life without ups and downs here
    below;
But mine have been mostly benevolent crosses,
  Where the balance came right, as the ledgers will
    show.

So in me He finds nothing but thankfulness truly
  That I am not like some who have wasted His gift,
That I never gave way to a passion unruly,
  And when things at the worst were, I always made shift

To believe in His providence; and I have seen it,
  For every thing throve with me well from the first;
I am sure not an hour of my life or a minute
  But He faithfully saw to my hunger and thirst.
But it all depends, sir, on doing your duty,
  And carefully laying your doubts on the shelf,
And keeping your head clear of women and beauty,
  To make it the best of all worlds—for yourself."

To him then, the Exquisite: "Ah! it is pleasant
  To meet, now and then, an exceptional case,
A man who is really content with his present,
  Content with himself, and his prize in the race:
Not that I think, now, you should be contented
  I could not, though I had your luck, sir, instead
Of the emptiest life that was ever invented;
  But I call no one happy, until he is dead.

You've not seen the end yet. The cup running over
   May be dashed from your lips, and its treasures
      all spilt:
Most likely it will; and your friend then and lover
   Will look on your trouble as if it were guilt.
We are playthings of Nature, and Nature is cruel;
   She mocks us with favours to break our hearts
      worse;
To-day, she adorns us with some precious jewel,
   To-morrow, the jewel of life is its curse.

We have pure thoughts of love, we have high
      thoughts of goodness,
   We glow with fine feelings, and call them divine.
While nature is raging in wrath, or in lewdness,
   And planning an earthquake, or twisting the spine.
And why has she made us so, but for the keen edge
   Which conscience can put on the pain we must
      bear?
And we fondly look on to a happy serene age,
   While she has made sure of its sorrow and care.

Oh your life has been filled full of mercies and
      blessings,
   Wife and children and all that your heart can
      desire;

Your God whom you trust has been kind and
    caressing,
And how can you praise Him enough and admire?
Well; I hope it may last, sir; but sometimes one's
    children
  Have broken the hearts that they once made
    so glad—
I don't say yours will; but it's rather bewildering
  When our mercies turn out the worst ills we
    have had.

You think it's all goodness that sends you your
    treasures;
And yet your heart sinks at a fall in consols,
And there is a bitter drop mixed in all pleasures,
  And there is a vague longing still in our souls:
Why can this Goodness not heartily give us
  What cannot be lost, and what fills up our
    peace?
And why does He grudge all at once to relieve us,
  And bid fear and trouble and sorrow to cease?

Was it Goodness that fashioned the tiger? and
    hollowed
  The fang of the cobra that bites in the dark?

And what was the fond line of thought which it
    followed
  When it planted the teeth in the jaws of the
    shark?
Or the love that created those lizards and dragons,
  And mail-clad the fishes, when earth was but
    slime!
It could wait through long æons for ploughshares
    and waggons,
  But for carnage must not lose a moment of time!

We blame our fierce soldiery lusting for battle,
  We number their slain with a horror aghast,
We mourn the waste land, without homestead or
    cattle,
  Through which the fell march of their armies has
    past;
Yet what have they done but what Nature is doing
  On a yet grander scale all the days and the
    years,
For she either is battling, or else is renewing
  Her strength for the war, with its woes and its
    tears.

Just look at the ants on their slave-stealing forays;
  What goodness and mercy impel them to go?

Or gaze on the tender young lambs in the corries
　　As the ravens scoop out their meek eyes in the
　　　　snow :
And perhaps it was love armed the midge and
　　　　mosquito
　　That curse the bright warm summer day to us all,
And the wasp and the hornet are owing to it too.
　　And the centipede hid in the old mossy wall.

Nay, but Nature is fierce, sir, and false too and
　　　　cruel,
　　And all through her realm there is war to the
　　　　knife,
All through her years runs the long deadly duel,
　　The constant unpitying battle for life.
And what is such life worth? and what of its
　　　　donor?
　　When each creature takes what advantage he may
Of cunning or sickness, and no laws of honour
　　Can stay the fierce hunger, or shelter the prey?

Oh, it's not so with man, is it? He has a higher
　　And nobler law which he is bound to obey;
Though sprung from the brute, it is his to aspire
　　To a grander and happier life than they!

A happy life!—gout-racked or tossing in fever;
   A noble life!—scrambling for pence in the mire;
Oh, you pity the poor Chartist cobbler or weaver,
   But you leave him for all that to pine by the
      fire!

And then, sir, what need of our huge grated prisons,
   Our gibbets and soldiers and batoned police,
And other the like most convincing of reasons
   In the best of all possible worlds like this,
But that the stronger would keep down the weaker.
But that the cunning would outwit the fools,
But that the poorer of us and the meeker
   Must needs be their victims, or else be their
      tools?

Well; but here is a manor-house, yonder a palace,
   Or a lot of trim villas—sure God must be good!
Ay; but what of the millions in closes and alleys
   Scant of all raiment and light, sir, and food,
And the babes that are suckled on whisky or fever,
   And the girls that ne'er knew a maiden's pure
      thoughts,
And the pains and the aches that the Bountiful
      Giver
   Dispenses as freely as dust and motes?

No, it is not worth living, this hard life of sorrow :
    But there is no other, and we must bear on,
Toiling to-day without hope of to-morrow,
    Weary and dull till the light is gone.
I once held with you, sir; trying to dream on,
    In spite of the facts, in a fool's paradise;
But if there's a deity, sure he's a demon
    Who wrings us with anguish, or tempts us with vice.

Well spoke the wise Greek in his tragic elation,
    As he pictured the brave heart Fate held in his mesh,
Hurling his scorn at the gods and salvation
    With the spikes of the Caucasus piercing his flesh.
High-souled the Greek was, moral and fearless,
    And his gods must do right ; or his soul would rebel ;
But we must be meek when our life is most cheerless,
    With a lie in our mouth saying, It is all well."

So they sat there—the two of them—talking and drinking,
    And eyeing the ruby light-gleam of the wine,
Well pleased with their talk, for they thought they were thinking,
    And each deemed that he did the secret divine;

And each took his bottle there pleasant and merry,
    And each with an easy mind then had his nod.
And which was the best judge of claret and sherry?
    And who of the twain was the farthest from God?

Oh best of all worlds for the selfish and shifty,
    Thou art not so good for the noble and true;
Oh life well rewarding the prudent and thrifty,
    How shall the Christ-spirit travail with you?
Oh worst of all worlds to the proud heart and faithless!
    And yet thou canst perfect the meek and the brave;
Strange, sorrowful life that in dying is deathless,
    Glory and mystery, found in a grave.

Evil the world is; Life a long battle,
    Wrestle with anguish, and warfare with sin,
Proving the heart of us, trying our mettle
    By troubles without us and terrors within;
And yet 'tis worth living, to-day and to-morrow,
    The life which God lived in the wealth of His love,
Life He made perfect in patience of sorrow,
    God-life on earth like the god-life above.

Deacon Dorat's Story.

This is the saw that cut him down,
   The last in our place that was hung in chains,
   Left to bleach in the suns and rains
On the gallow-hill of our Burgh town.

What he had done I remember not—
   Sheep-stealing, forgery, some offence
   Which rich men hate with a hate intense,
Nought can appease but to see the man rot.

Of course, in those days it was wrong to kill.
   Yet murder often escaped the rope;
   But for him there was not a gleam of hope,
Who wrote your name to a cheque or bill.

I say this because, though I am not aware,
  After all these years, what his crime might be.
  Had he wrought a murder, it's certain we
Would have left the corbies to pick him bare.

Yet it was not for that we cut him down;
  But the gallow-hill stood at the end of the Links.
  And it spoilt our game at the golfing rinks,
That ghastly thing with its grinning frown.

And we also thought they might hang, or shoot,
  Or head the living rogues, as they chose;
  But it was like a savage to punish those
Who were tried already, and dead to boot.

And it was not our kindly old Scotch Law
  Which hanged a man, and was done with him :
  It was only the English that left the grim
Corpse for the kite's and the raven's maw.

So we vowed to get the thing out of our way;
  We were young fellows, and apt to think
  In a wildish way o'er a drop of drink,
And the gallows, at any rate, spoilt our play.

A dismal night! I remember well
   The sullen moan of the restless sea,
   And the rain that plashed on hill and tree,
And how my heart thumped at the midnight bell!

Ugh! how the creature grinned and mowed,
   As if he knew what we were about,
   And thought that his airy perch without
Was better perhaps than a grave and shroud.

Now and then from the town we heard
   The night-watch call, but he came not near,
   And once we paused with a thrill of fear
At two or three notes like a singing bird.

What was it? where was it? Hushed with awe,
   We stood for a moment with bated breath;
   When tripping up to that loathsome death
Two merry boys and a girl we saw.

Wild black elf-locks, and wild large eyes,
   Came, weirdlike, tripping along the hill,
   Singing a merry song, until
They saw us there with a blank surprise.

L

"Come hither, now, children: what do ye,
   At midnight here, by the gibbeted dead?
   And are ye not fearful now, I said,
On the bleak bare hill of the gallows tree?"

"Nay," quoth the maiden straight and tall,
   "Why should we fear the peaceful dead?
   He is our father, sirs," she said;
"He is our father," said they all.

There was a lump, sir, rose in my throat,
   And there was a something that dimmed my sight;
   But I said, "Would you be glad this night,
If this your father again you got?"

"Mother will soon be here, they said,
   She is coming to curse the Law and the Judge,
   But there is no blessing that she will grudge
If you give us our father back instead.

"Lo! we will haste, and bid her come,
   Yea, we will haste, and drive the cart,
   For she will have drunk to cheer her heart"—
Then they hurried away and left us dumb.

So we cut him down; and an ugly job
  It was—may I ne'er do the like again,
  And we waited an hour, in the pelting rain,
Under the gallows that we did rob.

But the wild elf-locks, and the wild large eyes,
  And the tripping feet, and the eerie song,
  We looked for them, and we listened long;
Then laughed that we could have believed their lies.

We had cut him down; but what now to do,
  When we had him down, that puzzled us all,
  For we had not thought of his burial,
And it must be done before morning too.

We spoke of the river near at hand,
  But the thing would float there by and by;
  We thought of the sea where the tide was high,
But that would drift him again to land.

We could easily climb the Kirkyard wall,
  But the bedral slept near, wakeful, grim,
  And the crunch of a spade would waken him,
And a glance would tell him about it all.

Were ever men puzzled so much before
  By getting the thing they were fain to get?
  An' if it had been a burden of debt
It could not have loaded our spirits more.

We could not carry the creature home,
  We could not leave it upon the hill!
  Oh, but it's strange to get your will,
And wish you hadn't for days to come!

Then up by the winding sandy road
  A light cart passed by the shooting-butts,
  Jolting o'er hummocks, and creaking in ruts,
And came to the place where we still abode.

And with it a gipsy woman we saw,
  Straight and tall, with a manlike stride,
  With the three elf-children by her side,
And she came cursing the Judge and the Law,

Till she saw the Thing that lay at our feet,
  When she fell on the earth with a wild-beast cry,
  And clasped it, and kissed it, as we stood by
Silent, and hearing our own hearts beat.

Then they four lifted it from the ground,
  And laid it there on the donkey cart;
  Who shall tell me the thoughts of that wild heart—
For she too could love—when her dead she found.

"I am better at banning than blessing," she said,
  "But what of blessing my lips can give,
  May it be yours, while you breathe and live,
For that ye have given me back my dead.

"A rogue and a thief—what else could he be?
  But rogue or thief, lads, he loved us well;
  If he beat us too, as our backs can tell,
Who had a better right than he?

"Fear not the law shall find out what
  Ye have done this night; go home and sleep,
  Sure that your secret is buried deep;
I have them near by who will see to that."

She did not weep, and she did not pray,
  There was not a tremor in her tone,
  Yet she left us sobbing somehow alone,
When into the dark she strode away.

That day each street had its eager crowd;
  Who could have robbed the gallows tree?
  And the Council met, and the Provost, he
Spoke like a minister long and loud.

Oh how he fumed like a turkey-cock!
  We had done despite to the sacred law,
  We had robbed the gallows of half its awe,
We had given authority there a shock.

Nobody knew before in the town
  He could have been half so eloquent;
  And he was sure he was on the scent
Of the Law-defiers that "cut him down."

By and by they should find that he
  The law and its majesty would maintain,
  And hang the rogue in his chains again,
And make those rebels a sight to see.

They dredged the river, they searched the shore,
  They watched the kirk-yard, night by night,
  They questioned here and there, and quite
Lost their heads for a week and more.

Then one of us just threw out a hint,
   It must have been witchcraft—and it took
   With the ministers like a baited hook,
Who preached on it without let or stint.

That Sunday, sir, we learnt far more
   Of the Witch of Endor, and her arts
   For the making of dead men play the parts
Of living saints than for years before.

But the Provost, shrewd man, muttered Pshaw !
   Let the ministers preach and catechize ;
   If the devil had wanted such a prize,
What should he do with a workman's saw ?

But for me I heeded not what they said ;
   For it rung in my head there all day long,
   That eerie snatch of a gipsy song,
And "He is our Father, living or dead."

All the father she ever knew
   In earth or in heaven—that gruesome thing !
   And she had come up the hill to sing
Her song to him as she used to do !

O it was pitiful! but when I thought
   Of that wild night, and its madcap job,
   I could not be sorry that we did rob
The gallows, and gave them what they sought.

Better a quiet grave to fill,
   Where the grass is green, and the daisies grow,
   And the white thorn scatters its fragrant snow,
Than to mock their hearts on the Gallow hill.

And this is the saw that cut him down,
   And this is the hand that cleared the Links
   Of a thing that spoilt the golfing rinks,
Now and again, in our Burgh town.

The Poetaster.

There was a pathos in it, friend,
   Though you might smile, as I did too,
To see that pile of manuscript
So strangely from its cradle-crypt
   Brought suddenly to view.

Ah! there are things in this strange life,
   Which move us unto mirth, and yet
Behind the laughter there are tears,
And thoughts which in the after years
   Bring touches of regret.

And oft it is an accident
   Whether you chance to laugh or weep,
But when you call it back again
The laughter has a twinge of pain
   Which haunts you in your sleep.

He was a poor dull-plodding man,
  So poor he kept not even a bird
To cheer his solitude by song,
And voice for him the silent throng
  Of thoughts that find no word.

Nor dog, nor cat, nor bird had he,
  Nor wife nor child had ever come
To share the burden of his lot,
Which he endured and murmured not.
  In quiet patience dumb.

And now he lay there cold and dead,
  And none had watched to see him die;
Alone he had lived all his days,
Alone he passed from human ways
  Beneath the All-seeing eye.

There was a little loaf of bread—
  He had not died of hunger then—
A little fuel too, and oil,
And water in a can to boil
  If day should come again.

Which never came; and when we sought
   Through press and drawers for aught to give
Him decent burial with the dead,
As he had always held his head
   'Mong them that decent live,

Nor gold nor silver there was found,
   Nor plack nor penny; life had gone
Just as the little purse was spent,
Which lately had no increment
   From work that he had done.

It had just lasted out his time
   Through careful scrimping day by day;
He had no debt, he had no kin,
And there was nought to lose or win,
   When thus he went his way.

But for the money, vainly sought,
   In a moth-eaten trunk we found
A mass of manuscripts—a pile
Of papers writ in careful style,
   Some loose, some rudely bound.

Strange gatherings! scraps of every kind,
   Backs of old letters, envelopes,
Half-used account books, paper bags
Picked up among the ash and rags
   And refuse of the shops:

And every tattered scrap close writ
   With pen or pencil, as 'twould bear,
With verses on a hundred themes,
With pious arguments and dreams,
   All rhymed with patient care.

Oh no; he had no message, none,
   To wise or foolish, good or bad;
No prophet's burden-word he bore,
Which he must speak; and what is more,
   He never thought he had.

A silent soul, he went about
   His daily task, and every night
Back to his dingy attic came,
Nor dreamed about a coming fame
   Or setting this world right.

THE POETASTER.

None ever heard him hint a thought
   Of fancied greatness; never line
Of his competed for a place
In corners which small poets grace;
   He bottled it like wine.

But when his fellow labourers met
   With pipe and tankard at the inn,
He to his attic would retire,
And trim his lamp, and light his fire,
   And pen his verses thin;

And lived unto a good old age,
   And never begged a bit of bread,
And cheered his loneliness with these
Bald rhymes about the birds and trees,
   And living men and dead.

There is no sacred fire in them,
   Nor much of homely sense and shrewd:
Imperfect lines, imperfect rhymes,
False quantities, mistaken chimes,
   Yet all the feeling good.

There is no envy of the great,
　There's praise of patriot and saint;
If now the story have no point,
The reasoning now be out of joint,
　There is no vain complaint.

Hard toil it was for that hard hand
　To hammer out these limping lines,
Harder than handling spade or hod,
Or trenching ditch, or delving sod,
　Or picking in dark mines.

Yet night by night he must have writ
　His verse or two for forty years,
Long poems some, some meant for songs,
Some voiced the common people's wrongs,
　Some breathed his own sad fears.

But none had ever heard him say
　How the long evening hours were spent;
He never showed the rhymes he writ,
Nor tried to see their clumsy wit
　How it might look in print.

Enough for him the silent task,
   Enough to read the abortive rhyme,
Now pleased with this, now touched with that,
He knew not why; he knew not what
   Was pathos or sublime.

Strange passion! thus to jingle words,
   And hide them in a big old chest!
'Twas but some hours before he died
The last was written, and beside
   The rest in order placed.

Yet there was pathos in it, friend;
   I laughed a little on my road,
But the tears got the better soon,
It was so innocent to croon
   His bits of verse to God.

Parish Pastors

LONG AGO.

There were some five hundred, young and old,
Souls in the parish, when all were told,—
Cock-lairds upon the landward braes,
Scattered farmers, and cottar folk,
And the fishers who kept to their own old ways
In the village that huddled beneath the rock,
Where a sheltering cove made a safe retreat
For the brown lug-sails of their little fleet;
'Twas the only break in a stormy shore
Rock-girdled for ten good miles, and more.

Five hundred souls, and they did not care
Though neither a Bank nor a Post was there,

Nor Doctor to physic their mortal ills,
Nor Lawyer to draw their deeds and wills--
Ten miles off was a town where these
Might be had by them when they please ;
And farmers, going to market, brought
What letters there might be, now and then,
Which maybe had lain for a month, unsought,
Spotted with flies in the window pane.
Easily went the world with them,
They made no struggle its tide to stem,
But slumbered as in a quiet bay,
And heard its murmuring far away,
And grew their oats, and ground their bere,
And caught the fish, and fed the steer,
And noted the changes of the year.

But for the care of their souls they had
Of pious and learned pastors three;
Not that the way of their life was bad,
Or that more godly they sought to be
Than their neighbour-folk by the wild North Sea ;
But just that it had been so of old,
And they never thought to enlarge the fold,
And gather the flock together there
With ampler room and a freer air.

So had their fathers done, and they
Followed of course in their fathers' way.
And the pastors three with their scanty flocks
Of cock-lairds, farmers, and fisher folks,
Peacefully lived, as brethren should,
All of them busy in doing good,
Christening, wedding, and burying, each
After the manner his Church did teach,
And trying on Sundays truth to preach.

Dr. Boyack.

Low on a haugh, by the river side,
The homely Manse in its garden stood,
With a clump of grand old elms to hide
The rough-cast walls, and the paintless wood.
And close to it was the parish kirk,
But what it was there was nought to tell
Save only a belfry and tinkling bell,
Above its rough-cast rubble-work.
A humble Kirk, and a homely Manse
On the haugh among the trees and rooks;
Where the white-thorn hedges had grown, perchance,
Unpruned for the sake of the ricks and stooks,

For the stooks of corn and hay are more
Than a well-trimmed hedge to a household poor:
But they helped to make more wildly fair
The old Manse-garden breathing there
Of thyme and every sweet herb that grows,
And the pink, and wall-flower, and cabbage rose.
Oh, there the strawberry beds were good,
And the gooseberry bushes had golden fruit,
And the apple-tree boughs were stayed with wood,
They clustered so thick upon every shoot,
And the jargonelles on the gable hung
Sweet as honey the leaves among :
Just a garden for boys and girls,
Ne'er while they lived to be forgot;
And sunny faces and golden curls.
Flashed through its trees when the sun was
    hot—
Eight wild boys, and as many maids
In homespun dresses, with unkempt hair,
Laughed and sang in the grassy glades,
Or gathered the fruits of the garden fair,
And gladdened the minister's heart, but yet
They burdened it too with a fear of debt.

Easy-natured and kindly he,
Respectable always in every thing;

Nothing he did but it had the ring
Of cultured mediocrity;
In talents, in morals, in learned lore
Respectable ever, and nothing more.
No special mission had he to preach;
No special faculty his to teach;
Nor special power of the priestly art
Or to console, or move the heart;
There seemed no reason why he should be
God's servant there in the parish Kirk,
Instead of dealing out tape or tea,
Or driving the plough from morn to mirk,
Save that he read some Latin and Greek,
And wrote good words that were smooth and weak.
Yet he did his task in a patient way,
With doctrine solid, if stiff and cold,
Ready by day or by night to pray
With the sick or the poor that were in his fold—
Mostly the farmers and cottar-folk,
To all of whom, as they hung about
After sermon, the minister spoke
Of the weather and crops, and the sheep and *nowt*,
And their rheumatisms, and their girls and boys,
And all their commonplace griefs and joys.
No high ideal had he to raise

Their souls from the level of common ways,
Nor passion nor power to stir the mind
As with the rush of a heaven-born wind:
But well he knew all their homely lot,
Their joys and sorrows he ne'er forgot,
Could tell what came of the scholar son,
And where had the married daughter gone,
Had ever the fitting word on his lip,
And griped each hand with the proper grip:
That bound their hearts to him fast and true
As surest cords of love could do.
Little he read, and what he did
Was mostly sermons to "fang his pump,"
When it ran dry, and the weekly need
Rang in his head like a warning trump.
Yet though he made complaint that wealth
Of letters, alas! was not for him,
Being rich in children in hungry health,
I trow he was not a man to dim
His eyes with poring on musty books;
Far better he liked the cawing rooks,
The smell of the hay-field, and the talk
Of farming folk in a sauntering walk;
For what of learning he had was worn
Outside, like clothes of the proper trim,
But it never was truly part of him,

And now it was somewhat rent and torn.
He had not a doubt to trouble him,
And his faiths were only as corks to swim
Through life as easily as he might,
And net whatever might come his way;
And with the world he would not fight,
If he could only get through the day.
Yet he was reasonable, and shed
A sort of light too along his path,
Which not from the heavenly founts was fed,
Nor yet from the baleful fires of wrath:
It was somewhat earthly perhaps and cold,
And led not many into the fold,
But yet it did not lead astray,
If it only lit up half the way.
No lofty purpose in life had he,
No spirit earnest and brave and true
The glory and hope of God to see;
Nor yet a-craving for something new:
But he walked with them in the way they
    trod,
And talked with them of the things they knew,
And his speech was easy and natural too,
Save when he spoke of the things of God.
A wholesome nature, and fain to please;
Saintship in him had been like disease

Which he was ever upon the watch -
Though he hardly needed it—not to catch ;
For to be called Fanatic he
Dreaded like sin and misery.

Dean Duffus.

Down in the cove, where the fisher folk
Huddled beneath the lighthouse rock,
There was a dainty little Kirk
Of the old faithful mason-work,—
It might be the choir, or the pillared nave,—
With a bell that rung o'er the breaking wave,
And a great cross on the gable stood ;
And all within it was fair and good,—
Marble altar, and carven font,
And silver vessels, as were wont,
Under the great black holy Rood.

Long it had been but a ruin grey,
Roofless, and wasting in slow decay,
The mullions all from the windows gone ;
The carven niche, and the fine-scrolled stone
By nettles and long grass hid from view ;
And the font had been broken and overthrown,
And pillar and arch were crumbling too ;

And the cunning fox had made his lair,
And the rook and the jay had nestled there.
Some laid the blame upon Knox's wrath ;
Some held it was swept from the Covenant's path ;
Some charged it to Cromwell's Ironclads ;
And some to a raid of the Highland lads ;
But they who had searched the matter well
Read how a great Lord lost a bet,
And tore off the roof, and melted the bell,
And sold them to pay his gambling debt,
After the new Kirk was built away
Landward, far from the little bay.
And all agreed that a Kirk was there
From the days that the Culdee launched his boat,
And came with the voice of psalm and prayer,
And gospel true to the people brought
From the lone Isle of saints that lay
Where ghostly mists on the waters slept,
But God shone out of the mists by day,
And spake in dreams to them when they slept,
And ever their souls in quiet kept.

So the good Dean, when he came there,
Curate or priest, long years ago,
Loving a Kirk that was old and fair
As the ivy loves round its walls to grow,

Had clung to it with a longing heart,
And with his own hands cleared a part,
Casting out nettles and grass and earth,
Till he came to the pavement of solid stone,
And whatever of beauty he found, or worth,
He sought out its place, and fitted it on.
Then with his savings, year by year,
He mended a bit, and roofed it in,
Living himself on sorriest cheer
This trophy again for his Church to win:
And now it stood there fair to see
In lines of graceful symmetry;
A bell once more from the steeple rung,
And matin and vesper were daily sung,
And the organ pealed, and the common prayer
Was sweetly toned to the fishers there.
Yet all the wealth of his worldly gear
Was less than three score pounds a year.

Near by the Kirk was a cottage small,
With a red-tiled roof, and a white-washed wall,
A garden plot that was bright with flowers,
An old sun-dial to tell the hours,
Some carven stones that were broken quite,
And might not fit in their places right,

Yet were too sacred to be thrown
Among the rubbish of common stone,
With a green paling to fence all round,
These told where the Dean a home had found.
It was not other than all the rest
Of the fishermen's huts that there were seen,
Save only that it was neat and clean,
With an attic chamber for a guest:
But the Dean's own bed was in the wall,
Hid behind volumes, great and tall,
In the little room where he read and wrote,
And did the work that a pastor ought.

There on the shelves were folios piled;
There Benedictine fathers smiled
In snowy vellum, crimson-lettered—
These he said were his golden mines—
And high on the upper shelves were scattered
Big quartos too of the great divines,
And tables and chairs and floor were littered—
With books that were scored with scarlet lines;
For he was a classic ripe and good,
And loved the old wine in the seasoned wood,
But all translations were bottled and dead.
With an evil taste of the cork, he said.

The other room was a kitchen clean.
And there no woman was ever seen,
But once a day, about noon, his man
Lit up the fire for a little can—
If it were not a fast, and a fast, at least,
Came twice a week to this humble priest—
And made for him pulse or porridge sweet.
But the Church's Feasts had sodden meat;
And if a guest by chance was there,
There might be a glass of mildest ale;
And an evening pipe to soothe his care
Was the one luxury did not fail.
Yet was he healthy and strong, nor kept
Ever his bed for a day, or slept
After the dawn, but rose to pray
For his fisher lads in the stormy bay.

A tall, lean form with lank grey hair.
Bushy his eyebrows, and grey his eyes,
Deep sunk in a face that was pale and spare:
And he dressed in a threadbare lowly guise.
One apron had served him all his days,
His newest hat, it was ten years old,
His well-brushed coat had a shining glaze,
And his great thick shoes had been patched and
    soled;

White was his lawn on the Sabbath morn,
But half was darning, and all was worn
Into so fine a filament
It scarce could be handled without a rent.
Yet had he ever so stately an air
That rich and poor did understand,
Whatsoever his raiment were,
He was a man to hold command,
And none might slight him in all the land.

Old was the world in which he lived,
Old the evils at which he grieved,
Old were the things that most he cherished,
Old were his hopes too, past and perished.
He held that it was a sin to own
Other than Stuart to sit on the throne,
And still did his faith intact remain
Now that there was not a Stuart to reign.
Therefore a strict non-juror he
All the years of his youth had been,
Doing his constant ministry
In hidden ways, and in spots unseen,
Praying for him who in exile lay
"Over the hills and far away."
Now law and order he kept, 'tis true,
Giving to Cæsar Cæsar's due,

But the loyal heart that would have shed
Its blood for the kings of the ancient line,
Clung to the memories of the dead,
And the vanished rule of the Right divine.
He fasted still for the martyred Charles,
And him who perished on Magus moor,
And held that the Parliament men were
 carles,
The devil pricked on to delude the poor,
And that gallant Dundee did right to maul
The Westland Whigs who were rebels all.
But for the new world, and its ways,
And all the great hopes of the latter days,
Their science and its expanding views,
New-fangled craving for latest news,
And workmen striking for higher wage,
And all that mostly our thoughts engage—
For them he kept strictly a yearly Fast,
Each year bitterer than the last—
It fell when Culloden day begins—
And he called it the Fast of All the Sins.

So, true to his own ideal, there
He chaunted the psalm, and read the prayer,
And gathered the lore of ancient times
From Latin Fathers and Latin rhymes,

Till scholars came from far and near
This primitive Pastor to revere;
But hardly ever a point was found
Where he touched the life that went on around,
Moved it, or felt with it as it spoke,
Or heeded how its passions woke,
Or how its bubbles swelled and broke.

The Reverend Richard Rule.

Landward upon the rolling braes,
Wind-swept, and apart from the common ways,
Where once had stretched a moorland waste,
But now it was covered with grass and corn,
Another kirk on a height was placed
Among two or three pinetrees tempest-torn;
And Church of the Wilderness it was named,
Built for a prophet-pastor famed
For his doom-speaking words, and his stedfast
    faith,
When the wild dragoons were dealing death;
But he lived through the evil times, and saw
Though he would not allow, a better law;
And the bonnet lairds on the rolling braes
    Had been Cameron's men in the troublous days.

A plain square building, never meant
To be tricked with carnal ornament,
Rough in its stonework, and rude in its lines,
Grimly it stood by the ragged pines.

There ministered one who held his head
High as the Dean, and would not brook
King or Parliament, living or dead,
Unless the Covenant oath they took :
William or George, Charles or James,
Stuart or Guelph, it mattered not,
Nor what their characters, what their aims,
Or whence their claim to have rule was brought.
Whether from Bishop's anointing oil,
Or from the people who sweat and toil,
Or from a long ancestral line
Lapt in the dream of a right divine;
He would protest against the throne,
Unless the Covenant it would own,
For this was a Covenant Land, and bound
By solemn league to be holy ground
Where Papist, Prelatist, Sectaries all
Should ne'er have authority great or small.
Nor should Erastian preach the Word
Where the martyred saints of old were heard.

He was a small, brisk, cheerful soul,
Not a whit gloomy or morose,
Apt at telling a story droll,
Gay among brethren and jocose,
And hardly would he restrain his wit
When in grave Presbytery even they sit.
Yet in the pulpit he would groan
About the defections which he saw,
And that he would soon be left alone
Even as Elijah to stand by the Law,
And by the altar and truth of God,
For which our Fathers dyed the sod
Red with their own best blood, that we
Might have the gospel pure and free.
Then would his tremulous voice swell higher,
Like the sound of winds among trees that
 moan,
As though some Power did his soul inspire,
Nor even the Dean could so finely intone.

He, too, was a man of learning, skilled
In all polemics since Luther broke
Her sleep, and the Church from dreams awoke,
And wrath was kindled, and blood was spilled.
Well had he conned each mighty tome
Of Calvinist, Lutheran, Doctor of Rome,

And what the Philistine Prelate writ,
And how the Puritan-David hit
The boastful giant with sling and stone,
And struck down the mitre that wrecked the throne.
The faintest shade of Arminian error
Well could his watchful eye detect,
And he thundered at it, in wrath and terror,
For comfort there of the Lord's Elect.
So he deemed he must faithful be
Unto the little flock that he
Tended and fed amid sore distress
In the lonely Church of the Wilderness.

Stronger he than the other two,
Learning and talent he did not lack;
Yet were there some things he could do
From which their souls would have shrunken back.
He was not so noble, I reckon, as they,
At least, he could stoop to a meaner way,
And did not feel it, but made a jest
Of that which had broken their soundest rest.
For the wee cock-lairds that were his flock,
They were as hard as the flinty rock;
And minded to have their gospel cheap,
Letting him sow if themselves might reap;

And, maybe, dealing with them had been
The blunting of feelings that once were keen;
And maybe the children's hungry cry
Quenched the gleam of his wrathful eye.

Five hundred souls, when all were told,
Dwelt in the parish, young and old,
Well shepherded surely by pastors three
Who lived together in amity,
And had no quarrels, nor sought to rob
Each other's folds of a sheep or lamb,
And lived, far off from the noisy mob,
In a world of their own that was full of calm.
Yet what could they do for the landward folk,
Or the fishers beneath the lighthouse rock?
What help to their warfare could they bring?
What light to shine on the darkening road?
What song could they give their hearts to sing
When burdened with sorrow or death or—
    God?
What gospel had they to raise the soul
Above the weather and crops and beeves,
And spur them to run for the grander goal
In the world beyond these falling leaves?

Respectable one, and easy-hearted,

He went about in a kindly way;
One lived in a world that had long departed;
And one was eager the slain to slay;
Meanwhile the people grew their oats,
And mended lines and nets and boats,
And made their malt, and brewed their ale,
And drank at wedding-feast and fair,
And harvest-home, and auction-sale;
And at the funerals took their share
Of heavy wines and waters strong,
As they bore the dismal bier along.
But there were mothers that were not wives,
And there were widows that tired of weeping,
And there were prodigals wasting lives,
And sorrowful hearts that lay unsleeping,
Through weary nights long vigil keeping.
And they had their thoughts about life and death,
And sin and mercy and God and faith;
And now and then from the world without
There came to their souls strange wafts of doubt,
And things that were not in the catechism;
But how to deal with them no one knew
They dreaded heresy, error and schism,
But wist not what of these thoughts were true,
Or what, if they were, they ought to do:

For the three good pastors kept their road,
And lightened not any one of his load.

Now, times are changed; there are not many more
Souls in the parish than were of yore,
Yet the pastors three have grown to four;
And their thoughts are run in a sharper mould,
And a spirit is there which was not of old.
It may be, their faith in God is more,
But they have not the same faith in each other;
It may be, they love Christ as before,
But they walk not so lovingly now together:
And mostly they build partition wall,
Not the wall of a larger fold;
For that which is common alike to all,
That of little account they hold.
And yet a milder gospel tells
Of love that in the Father dwells,
And sweeter strains of praise are sung,
And bells in graceful spires are rung.
And they all walk in stricter ways,
And they all spend laborious days.
For life is there, and that is good,
Though it be young life in its selfish mood—
Life is there, with its warmth and power,
Its yearning hope, and its eager strife,

Its thought unfolding like a flower,
Its craving still for a fuller life,
Its futile effort, its failing faith,
Its fresh revival and confidence,
Its error too, like a misty wraith,
Ghost of some old forgotten sense—
Life with its loves, and hates, and fears,
Its wondrous joys, and its bitter tears,
Its follies, blunders, useless fights,
Its brooding shadows, and mystic lights:
Life has broken the slumberous spell,
And it is not all good,—yet it is all well.

Amory Hill.

I.

Does any one know about Amory Hill?
   What an unrestful mind she had,
   Questioning everything, good and bad,
Subtle in thought, and firm of will!
   Beautiful, too, in her way: but what
   Ever could come of a girl like that?

Oh, you remember the large grey eyes;
   What a keen look in them did lie,
   Fain to be told the reason why
We ever held anything true or wise!
   And say what you might, she would still find out,
   Somehow or other, a ground for doubt.

Under the Word she must see the Thing.
  Never content with the neatest phrase;
  The coin might be of the ancient days,
But still she must try if it truly ring,
  And bite it too with her dainty teeth,
  For it might look well, and be false beneath.

No matter how old a lie might be,
  Age, she said, could not make it true;
  No matter though truth be fresh and new,
It was the pleasanter sight to see,
  Like a fresh star your eyes behold,
  Where never a star had been seen of old.

Liked! how could she be liked, a girl
  Who'd squat her down in a quiet nook,
  Out of the way, with a folio book,
With all the rest of us there in a whirl
  Of work or talk? And she did not heed,
  If only we left her at peace to read.

Of course, her doubts and her questions tried
  Every one's patience, more or less,
  And the older folk, when they felt the stress,
Were fain their ignorance to hide,
  And sent her off, with a sharp rebuke,
  Back again to her folio book.

Somehow she never took it ill,
   Whatsoever you chanced to say;
   But not in the least did it change her way;
She soon had another question still:
   Never the same one twice, for now
   She would puzzle it out by herself somehow.

What could come of a girl like that,
   Who would not walk on the common road,
   Who fretted at bearing the common load,
And did not know what she would be at,
   And was not sure of the common creed,
   And gave not her dress a moment's heed?

Oh, Amory Hill! Amory Hill!
   And yet how good she was and nice,
   Scorning a meanness, and hating a vice,
With a brave true heart and a patient will,
   Loving the truth, and not afraid!—
   What has come of the grey-eyed maid?

Amory Hill.

II.

I thought you had heard of Amory Hill:
   It made at the time a mighty stir,
   But nobody now-a-days thinks of her.
We wonder at nothing, good or ill,
   After two or three days are past—
   That is enough for a comet to last.

Amory grew, as you might expect,
   From a doubting, questioning, restless elf
   To a woman who brooded by herself
About the Church, and the Lord's Elect,
   About the fate of the quick and dead,
   Doubting the moré, the more she read.

At a Revival some one got
   A hold of her for a little while;
   And she sang their hymns with an angel's smile,
And tried to live on their shallow thought;
   But back the questions came, and then
   Oh, she was deep in her doubts again.

She writ a Book that I tried to read,
   But could not tell what it was about—
   Just like thoughts that she had thrown out
Into the darkness of thought and deed,
   And heard them in the silence roll
   Back again on her yearning soul.

Poor girl! she wandered, here and there,
   From pastures green where the grace was rife,
   Seeking the Way and the Truth and the Life,
And finding but shadows and dim despair,
   Till she came to the perilous brink of Faith,
   Beyond which lieth the realm of death.

Star after star had all gone out,
   Darkest night was on all her sky;
   And moaning as one who is ready to die,
Ah, me! she said, Must I live without
   God and His Christ and the hope divine,
   That erewhile gladdened this life of mine?

Then one laid hold of her, drew her back
   From the dismal gloom of that deadly brink,
   Told her that now she must cease to think,
And then no wisdom her soul should lack;
   If to the Church she would only bow,
   It would do all of her thinking now.

Bland his speech was, and mild his look;
   Was he an angel come from heaven
   To save the soul that was tempest-driven
There where in terror and pain it shook?
   And what had all of her thinking brought,
   Except despair of all certain thought?

So straightway into his arms she fell,
   Cast away Reason, and swallowed the Creeds,
   Mumbled her aves, and counted her beads,
And said it was good in peace to dwell
   With Nuns who had not a thought in their head—
   But is it the peace of the living or dead?

She does much good to the sick and poor,
   Going about in that quaint odd dress
   With the little book which her fingers press:
But then she did quite as much good before,
   For Amory Hill was always sweet,
   And came like a sunbeam along the street.

Amory Hill.

III.

Who would know me for Amory Hill,
    Once the plague and the tease of School,
    Querying lesson, and breaking rule?
And yet I fear I am Amory still,
    Under the white cap and the hood
    Of the patient merciful Sisterhood.

I've tried, till I think there is no use trying
    To be anything other than I was made;
    I've sought the light, and I've sought the shade,
I've crushed my thought, when it rose defying,
    I've nursed submission, and fondled pain,
    Yet ever the thoughts come back again.

Weary, I'm weary; what shall I do?
  Oh, will that chatter of theirs not cease?
  Here I had hoped to have quiet peace
In the daily round of duties true,
  And the tranquil hymn, and the whispered prayer.
  Freed from the burden of trouble and care.

Once I wrestled, in earnest thought,
  With weighty problems of truth and faith,
  With the high issues of life and death,
And what we should not do, what we ought:
  But here our wrestle is not to think—
  Can it be more sinful to see than wink?

Does God, indeed, mean that we should not bear
  The burden of thought? or fashion a life
  Of peace, instead of the noble strife
Inspiring ever the soul to dare,
  And make fresh conquests, if it may,
  On the realm of darkness, day by day?

Oh! but this is rebellion, this is sin:
  So they tell me, and I have tried
  To crush it out, and have done, beside,
Many a penance for letting it in.
  But is it sinful? and can it be right
  To close the shutters, when God is Light?

This is the hour when they sit and talk,
   Oh, such nothings! and not without
   Touches of malice too, all about
What they saw in the daily walk
   To visit the sick and the poor, when they
   Looked on the world and its wicked way.

But why is the world more wicked than they?
   They were silly girls ere they took the vow,
   And they're just as silly sisters now.
Ribbons and gawds may be put away,
   And love and marriage be counted shame,
   Yet heart and mind may be still the same.

How should they differ from what they were?
   Hear! how they chatter as school girls do,
   And gossip about the folk they knew,
And who was married, and who was there:—
   I blame them not, if they did not blame
   The world as wicked for doing the same.

Are all the people who try to do good
   As little-minded as those I've known?
   Ere I came here, how I used to groan
At Dorcas meetings in angry mood!
   And the District Visitors need, I'm sure,
   Quite as much visiting as the poor.

Oh, how I shrank from the vulgar talk,
   The fuss, and the hard mechanical way
   Of saving so many souls a day
By dropping tracts in a morning walk !
   Not so, I said, would the work be done
   Here by the consecrated Nun.

But here or there, it is all the same,
   The talk alike, and the fuss and fret,
   And the vulgar methods of clearing debt,
And the mechanical ways and lame
   For doing of spiritual work, without
   The faintest thought what you are about.

And then this drilling of hands and lips !
   So many hours of work a day,
   So many hours to praise and pray,
All of our time cut into snips,
   And just as you get your mind in swing,
   There goes the bell with its ting, ting, ting !

Was I mistaken in coming here?
   Was it a hasty step I made?
   I am still free to go back, 'tis said ;
And I was not meant for a Nun, I fear.
   But they are all pleased with their happy lot,
   And what would they think if they knew my
      thought ?

It's nonsense what people were wont to say
   About the misery vows may bring,
   About the hearts that are suffering,
And the glad bright youth as it wastes away;
   There is nothing to waste, for they have no mind
   Nor heart nor passion of any kind.

And yet I feel that I am not free.
   Oh, the subtle threads that are wound
   About us here till our souls are bound,
And there's nothing for it but just to be
   As silly as all the rest, and make
   A merit of it for Jesus' sake.

I gave up my former life in dread
   Of the rush of thoughts into my soul,
   Terrible as the waves that roll
Over the weary swimmer's head;
   But now if I leave this, it will be
   In scorn of its dull vacuity.

Ay, if I leave it! but dare I go?
   Do I not know what would be said
   Better it were to be lying dead
Than pine away with a poison slow
   Of lies that would tingle in every vein,
   And break the heart with a nameless pain?

Ah! rebel nature could not endure
　The vacant mind and the weary day,
　The effort to keep all thought away,
But for the work 'mong the sick and poor :
　It is among them that I find my good,
　If they would not pain me by gratitude.

Miss Bella Japp.

TO HER YOUNG MINISTER.

Speak out, speak out!
We are all hungering, sir, for truthful words
    Of faith or doubt;
And we are weary of all mocking-birds
    Who would be dumb
If they might eat their meat, and do no more;
    And only come,
And sing again what we have heard before,
And grind again the same tune at the door
    To get their crumb.

Oh yes, yes, yes!
We have much talk, we have abundant speech
    In Rhetoric dress—
Thin thready talk that has no truth to teach;
    Poor echoes sent
From rock-like brains that barren are of thought:
    No nutriment
On which a soul may live is to be got
From echoes which are shadows, and give not
    The least content.

    Just speak out that
Which God gives you to live on day by day;
    And say not what
The people round about would have you say—
    Oh I could preach,
If they would let me, if I had a sphere!—
    If you would reach
The hearts of others, listen first and hear
What your own heart is saying, and speak it clear
    To all and each.

    Take not your words
From pulpit, platform, or from parliament;
    Just take the Lord's—
The words which from His lips to you are sent,

  Which few desire,
But all believe, whether they will or no :
  And for no hire
Proclaim them from the housetops where you go,
And cry aloud because they burn and glow
  In you like fire !

  What ! man, you talk
Of living by the gospel you proclaim !
  Well, if you walk
So as to glorify the Lord's great name,
  You shall have meat
Enough—the meat He gave to His own Son,
  And that was sweet.
" Not muzzle the ox ! " what harm that text has done,
Just making lazy " nowt " of many a one
  For meat to eat !

  I've gone to Kirk
Sixty years now since first with Jenny, nurse ;
  And what a work
I've heard them make about the Fall and Curse,
  Imputed sin,
Imputed right, imputed everything,

  Meanwhile within
The Devil who had us in his grips would sing,
" Impute away ! that's just the way to bring
  My bairns in."

  Now don't you spin
Notions and crotchet-things like that about
  Imputed sin,
When sin's a fact whereof there is no doubt;
  As you can see
Flaunting at every corner its disgrace
  Or misery,
And in the " Publics " running a hot race,
Ay! and at Kirk too smirking in the face
  O' the Pharisee.

  Then speak out, man ;
Out with it plain, the Devil is in the town,
  And what we can,
That, with God's help, we must, to put him down :
  Oh, fools may scoff,
But he laughs last who truth has on his side :
  Hell's not far off
Where dead folk are ; it's at your very side,
And souls drop in as balls are made to slide,
  I' th' holes at golf.

   There are the holes,
And here's the Devil's game, and well he plays;
   For thoughtless souls
Come dropping in, with some bit pleasant phrase,
   Each hour o' the day.
An easy job he's had this many a year,
   For it's poor play
We've had against him; God's been ill served here,
And it's been like to drive me mad to hear
   Their feckless way.

   But you have come
Fresh and hot-hearted, as I hear, from College,
   Freighted like some
Others, no doubt, with tons of useless knowledge.
   But, O my man,
It's not your metaphysics that we need
   Watery and wan;
Just take the Book, and with your own eyes read,
And drop the spectacles of an old-world creed
   About "The Plan."

   And preach right out
And pray; I do not mean to stamp the floor,
   And sweat and shout;
God is not deaf that you should need to roar:

But take our sin
Right by the throat, and call it by its name,
    Nor mind the din
The Devil will raise because ye spoil his game,
Or Pharisee because he's put to shame,
    Turned outside in.

Pick ye no words
To tickle itching ears with rhetoric:
    They have the birds
To sing to them if that is what they seek:
    It's dainty phrase
And mincing speech have been our very death
    These many days,
As in the Kirk we sought not truth and faith,
But tricks of art to hear with bated breath,
    Like fine stage plays.

Be strong and true;
Hold up our sins that we may see them bare,
    And hold up too
The Cross both to believe it, and to share
    Its pain and loss,
Should sorrow fill our cup unto the brim:

      For on the Cross
We see the glory as the eye grows dim,
Only we're fain to hand it on to him,
      Who clasped it close.

      Believing much
The Cross, that it is all our help and hope,
      We will not touch
It with our finger, fain to let it drop;
      And therewith cease
The grace and bliss and riches that it brings,
      And all increase;
Meanwhile we sing about the angels' wings,
And soothe the sickly conscience as it stings,
      And call this Peace.

The Village Philosopher.

He kept the village school—some score
　Of boys and girls, with little primers;
Their fathers he had taught before,
　Had called their mothers "idle limmers":
For well he liked to give hard names,
　But still in blandest accent spoken;
They never spoilt the children's games,
　Nor yet by them their heads were broken.

He had been village "merchant" once,
　But had not prospered in that calling;
A trade, he said, for any dunce,
　To be a ledger overhauling:
A silly, mindless business, he
　Was heard in very scorn to mutter,
To barter cloth and combs and tea
　And spades and rakes for eggs and butter!

For he was a philosopher,
   And such with trade make no alliance;
They said that even the minister
   Was puzzled with his views of science:
He knew the hour of the Eclipse,
   He made the Kirk a ventilator,
And could have sailed the biggest ships
   Across the line of the Equator.

Before the school door he had reared
   A pillar-stone and true sun-dial;
And in the window there appeared
   For weather glass a wondrous phial,
Its neck was partly ground, and then
   'Twas hung, mouth-downward, filled with water;
And if it dropped, there would be rain,
   But if it shrunk, the clouds would scatter.

He had a glass that showed the moon
   Whose mountains looked like inky blotches,
He had a box that played a tune,
   When rightly touched at certain notches;
He had a round electric wheel
   Could give a shock to all the village,
That made their elbows ache, and feel
   As tired as with a hard day's tillage.

He beat the smith—until he drank—
　At working cures on sickly cattle;
For when he came to byre or fank,
　The sight of him was half the battle:
In very fear the ewes grew well
　The moment that they smelt his potions,
And cows to healthy sweating fell
　To see his poultices and lotions.

So blandly as he pinched his snuff
　When he did horse or bullock handle;
So careful as he mixed the stuff
　By light of flaring lamp or candle;
So wisely as he would discourse
　Of Pleuro, Foot-and-Mouth, or Staggers,
And if the stubborn brutes grew worse,
　He glared at them with looks like daggers.

O little village-world that hast
　Thy prophets, watched with faith and wonder,
Stoutly believed in to the last
　In spite of failure, loss and blunder,
What art thou but the world in small?
　And what its prophets more than thine are?
Perhaps an inch or two more tall,
　But hardly even a shade diviner.

Altnacraig.

THE HIGHLAND HOME OF PROFESSOR BLACKIE.

Fair within and without,
Meet home for a sage and poet,
With the pine-clad red crags all about,
And the islanded sea below it;
Behind, is a ridgy hill,
And a burn leaps down the brae,
Where the sleepy clack of a little mill
Low-pulses through the day.

Fair without, but within
Is a rarer nobler beauty—
Womanly grace the heart to win,
And patient doing of duty;

And manly thinking and wise,
And lore of the ancient times,
And a free true soul that hath no disguise,
Still singing its careless rhymes.

Without and within, all fair,—
The form alike and the spirit—
He blithe and gay as the bird of the air,
She calm in her modest merit;
A self-assertive Greek,
Brisk to reason or jest,
Espoused to a Roman matron meek
And patient and self-suppressed.

Green Kerrera lies below,
You can see the green tower of Dunolly;
Lismore is green where the white ships go
Sailing by Appin slowly,
There are clouds on the hills of Mull,
And the mist over Morven streams;
And the heart of the Celt, like his day, is dull,
Or its lights but the fitfullest gleams.

O hills of Appin and Lorn,
And green foam-girdled islands,
And pools where the rushing streams are born
That sing to the lonely Highlands;

Dear to this friend of the Gael
Are loch and stream and Ben,
And the eerie legend and song and tale
That haunt the brachened glen.

Elf-like his locks and grey,
That wave o'er a Greek-like beauty—
Tokens of wisdom ripe, whose day
Was spent in Love and Duty;
But the spirit is gay and young
As in its dewy morn,
And ever the bird-like song is sung
As the fresh new thought is born;

Bird-like song from the hour
That fresh as the sun he rises,
Song in the mist and the flying shower,
Song when the light surprises,
Song on the lonely road,
Song in the thronging street;
Ever singing his thoughts to God,
For his thoughts are pure and sweet.

And whether of Clachan he speaks
Crumbling in dell of the Forest,
Or the rich full life of the grand old Greeks,
Or Him whom thou surely adorest,

The torrent of speech high-wrought,
It may be with froth on it,
Is ever a power too of generous thought,
With flashes of sparkling wit.

Now fatefullest tales are told
From Æschylus' tragic pages;
Now Plato and Goethe converse hold
Across the years and the ages;
Or Duncan Ban and the deer
Sweep down the rocky dell,
And burning pleas from his lips you hear
For the Celt he loves so well.

O haunt of the good and wise,
How oft have thy walls resounded
With eloquent pleas for the Celt that lies
By a sordid life surrounded,
Or with grief that his soul's true health
Should yield to the bigot's spell,
Or the meaner sway of vulgar wealth
That lords the hill and the dell!

Beautiful home of truth!
Shall we taste no more thy gladness,
Thy mirth with the innocent bloom of youth,
Thy wise and thoughtful sadness?

Shall we sit no more at thy board
As in the bright old times
With the lightsome jest, and the grave good word
And jets of dainty rhymes?

Farewell! the sea will beat
On thy brown rocks, crisply foaming,
And friends will sit on the far-viewed seat,
And talk in the golden gloaming;
But not such talk as we
Under the red pines had,
And, I think, I shall never more care to see
The place where I was so glad.

Cobairdy.

An old Scotch house, only one room wide,
    But four storeys high, with "a turnpike stair,"
That corkscrewed up a round tower on its side,
    With the outhouses, made three parts of a square:
A quaint coat-of-arms o'er the big-nailed door
    Had roughly been carved on a red sand stone,
And the gate to the square, which the same arms bore,
    Was arched overhead with a whale's jawbone.

The laird was a squat, little, hard-featured man,
    Something deaf in the hearing, and bowed in the legs,
Careful to waste nought, and get all he can
    For his oats and his bere, and his butter and eggs;

His mother lived with him in the kitchen there,
  For the parlour was draughty, and the dining room grim,
With no sort of comfort, the laird would declare,
  From portraits of old lairds that glowered down at him.

For some of them had red coats, and whips in their hand,
  Some, gay powdered heads and lace-ruffles fine,
And the red coats and ruffles meant acres of land,
  The laird could not think of, and cheerfully dine;
Yet the "Madams" were worse, with their head-tires and frills
  And satins, every yard of which had cost him dear;
For the clothing of their backs they had stript half his hills,
  And they were not like his mother for all their fine gear.

Rarely in the parlour, then, Cobairdy would sit,
  And never in the dining room, for that made him glum
To think how his forbears, men of little wit,
  Had parted with his acres for all time to come;

Racing and dressing and rattling at the dice,
  To rob him of half his bonny green hills,
Drinking and card-playing, and dabbling in vice,
  Till there was little left him but wadsets and bills.

So each night by the big kitchen fire he was seen,
  Where an oil-cruse and rushwick bleared through the reek,
He and his mother, with a draught-board between,
  Playing a long game would last near a week:
'Twas a saving of fire, and a saving of light
  And twice as much comfort, and half as much care;
And as for the game, if he lost in a night
  A penny to his mother, it was neither here nor there.

And day after day, with the sickle or the flail,
  Or the harrow or the plough he would toil, and not tire;
And night after night, his mother would not fail
  To set forth the draught-board beside the peat-fire;
Only on the Sundays, when they came from the Kirk,

And saw to the kye, and their fodder and their drink,
For the draughts they had "Boston" to read in the mirk,
And maybe o'er his pages would get just a wink.

Few were their words as they sat there alone,
　With the "lass" at her wheel, for no idleness was there;
And five and forty years now had thus come and gone,
　And the gear was aye growing, but the laird had grizzly hair;
Then his old mother sickened in the fall of the year
　When most she was needed as the long nights came,
And before the oak leaves were yellow all and sere
　He laid her in the Kirkyard with the rest of his name.

He laid her in the Kirkyard, and turned round his head,
　With a lump in his throat and a tear in his eye,
And thanked us for the honour we had shewn to the dead,
　And also he was glad that the day had been dry;

Could his mother but have known, the house had
   been right
His friends to receive as they surely ought to be,
And a proud woman she would have been that night
   To witness the respect of such a good company.

Then he took off his hat, and took from its crown
   A yard of red cotton, and bowed to us low,
Cried Gee! to the cart horse, and then sat him
   down
   Just where the coffin lay a little while ago;
And home came the poor laird, and went to the
   byre,
   And patted brown Crummie, his old mother's pet,
And stared at her hens, and her ducks in the mire,
   And vowed they should live, though they brought
   him in debt.

What could he do then? He tried for a time
   "The Fourfold State" of the children of men;
Good were the words, and the doctrine was prime,
   But it was a week day, and who could read then?
Not one good thought got he into his mind
   Of all that the good man tried hard to say.
And the more that he read, the more he grew blind,
   And oh but his old heart was "dowie and wae."

At last, looking round to "the lass" at her wheel,
   "Jeanie," he said, "will ye bring your stool near?
My mother's awa, but I think she would feel
   Better pleased if I went on as when she was here.
I've tried hard to read, but instead of the book,
   I see her old face, Jeanie, there where she sat,
And how, when she gave me a check, she would look—
   And we had not half finished the game we were at."

So the laird and his Jeanie sat down by the fire,
   With the cruse and the rush-wick to light up their play;
And she played her game well both in kitchen and byre,
   For Crummie grew sleek and Cobairdy grew gay.
And now she's the "leddy," as braw as the best,
   And sits in the parlour, and dines in the hall,
And her picture is hung by the laird's, with the rest
   Of the red coats and farthingales high on the wall.

Donald Toshach.

HIGHLAND LAND IMPROVER.

Big and burly and jolly and strong,
  Nineteen stone if he weighs a pound,
Yet as he strides, with his gun, among
  The corries and hills where the game is found,
  How light is his step o'er the heathery ground!

For his wind is sound, and his heart is gay;
  There's a dash of Norse blood in that light-haired Celt,
And his enterprise, and his dashing way
  He got from the Vikings of old that dwelt
  In the ships or the Brochs where the sea is smelt.

Great is his laughter, and needs but the half
   Of a joke to set it in roaring trim;
It is not the laughter that makes you laugh,
   Yet you would give something to laugh like him,
   For it seems to go rolling through every limb.

Shrewd at an argument, always keen,
   Celt-like, to reason of things divine,
Yet not, like the Celt, upon faith to lean,
   And pelt you with Scriptures line upon line;
   For texts to him are like sips of wine:

So he goes groping half in the dark,—
   Half in the dark, but he swears it is day—
Like one in a deep mine working stark,
   By a flickering lamp that shoots its ray,
   And shows the dark, if it shows the way.

But his strength is in action, in setting the folk
   Road making, bridge-building, planting trees,
Draining the marshes, and blasting the rock,
   Or reaping the harvest of the seas,
   Making the idlest busy as bees.

Watch him sitting on some grey stone,
   And overlooking the moorland brown;

What are his thoughts as he broods alone?—
  Of forests where now only heather is grown,
  And homesteads and mills, when it shall be his own.

" Yonder the mansion shall stand on its lawn,
  The hills shall be covered with larch and pine,
Here shall the flowering shrubs glow in the dawn,
  And the wasted torrents shall all combine
  To be a power and a slave of mine.

"God made no part of his earth to lie
  Waste as this is, with idle men
Watching the wild birds as they fly,
  Or red deer cropping the brachened glen,
  Or the salmon seeking the streams again.

"The corn may mildew, alas! on the field,
  And the hay lie wasted there where it grew;
Yet something there is which the land should yield,
  Something there must be for man to do
  Other than sport the whole year through."

Then will he buy a big lump of the shire,
  And men from the isles will come at his call,
To trench it, and fence it with stone and wire,
  Five hundred Islesmen strong and tall,
  Able workers at ditch and wall.

And slicing it up into small estates,
　　Planning houses and carriage-ways,
And winding paths with their wicket gates,
　　And planting thick on the hills and braes,
　　He toils through the sunny summer days.

Neighbours laugh at him, call him mad,
　　Prophesy death to his million trees,
Mock at his schemes, and are almost glad
　　Of any mishap that they can seize
　　To shew they were right in their auguries.

Till some day, lo! the five hundred men
　　Shoulder their picks, and march away
Back to their Western Isles again;
　　But twenty freeholders come, and they
　　Pitch their tents, for they mean to stay.

They love not idle folk there to see,
　　But they pay for work with their crowns and groats;
And they would have people strong and free
　　With kindlier crofts, and warmer cots,
　　And they are many—and they have votes.

But steeped in pride from the toe to the crown,
    Steeped in debt too up to the lip,
The neighbours askance at them look and frown,
    And try to hold on with a firmer grip,
    Lest from their hands the County slip.

But not for that does he toil and scheme ;
    What cares he for their party wars.
Could he but rouse them from their dream
    To care for the people, and heal their scars,
    And grow what Nature not debars?

But what they want is a solitude,
    A land that hath no neighbour folk,
Nor any work for the common good,
    But only a desert of bog and rock,
    Where the antlered stag and his hinds may flock.

" For deer and gilliedom are our curse,"
    So he vows in his stormy way,
" Making the lazy clansman worse,
    As he lives on the thriftless Saxon's pay
    With two months work, and ten of play."

Then will he turn and say, " 'Tis time
    I made a nest for myself at last ;

I have been changing soil and clime
   Only for others, but that is past;
   Where shall my own lot now be cast?"

Yonder a waste and lonely land
   Of bog and rock by a spreading lake :
There shall a goodly mansion stand,
   And glade and garden he will make,
   And all the hills into leafage break.

Yet when he looks on his finished home,
   Garth and forest and mansion too,
How shall he spend the days to come,
   Now there is nothing for him to do?
   Ah! he must find out something new.

Fair is the house beside the lake,
   And it rings with the voices of child and guest :
But there his pleasure he cannot take,
   It is no pleasure for him to rest ;—
   Making a new world still is best.

Sell it off for a rocky isle;
   There will he fashion a busy life ;

Bleak as the land is, it shall smile
  For ragged children and drudging wife,
  For there the wealth of the sea is rife.

Oats will not ripen, and barley fails,
  But the grass in the glens is green and sweet,
And the Lochs shall gleam with the fishers' sails,
  And the coves shall smile with houses neat,
  While the flocks in the glen shall browse and bleat.

O Rocky Isle in the western sea,
  Rouse thee on every cape and bay ;
Now listless slumber is not for thee,
  But curing and coopering all the day,
  And launching of boats on the ocean spray.

Oh for a hundred such as he !
  They tell me he will be ruined soon :
Pity ! and yet his work will be
  Stirring and brisk as a merry tune,
  E'en should he wane like a waning moon.

Industry has its martyrs too,
  And one might die in a worser cause ;

Yet do I hope he will live to view
  A people living by wholesome laws,
  And thriving homes where the sea-gull was.

For his brain is shrewd, and his schemes have thriven,
  As schemes never throve on these hills before ;
And why should he miss of the blessing of heaven,
  Now that his wits and his skill are more?
Oh, your prophets of evil are fain to prate
  If you scratch but the moss from their altar stones ;
But what do they know of the Gods and Fate,
  More than old wives from their aching bones?

Iona.

Lone, green Isle of the West,
Where the Monks, their corracle steering,
Could see no more, o'er the wave's white crest,
Their own loved home in Erin;
Shrouded often in mist,
And buried in cloud and rain;
Yet once by the light of a glory kissed,
Which nothing can dim again!

O'er tangled and shell-paved rocks
The white sea-gulls are flying;
And in the sunny coves brown flocks
Of wistful seals are lying;
The waves are breaking low,
Hardly their foam you trace;
All hushed and still, as if they know
This is a sacred place.

The diving guillemot
Is preening his dappled feather:
The great merganser shows his throat,
Red in this summer weather;
And bathed in a tremulous light
Are minster, cross, and grave,
That call up the past with a spell of might,
To tell of the meek and brave.

No fitter day than this
To look on thy mystic beauty,
And brood on memories of the bliss
Of faith and love and duty,
Of the hours of quiet prayer,
Of the days of patient toil,
Of the love that always, and everywhere,
Burned like a holy oil.

O lone green Isle of the West,
So oft by the mist enshrouded,
I have seen thee to-day in thy quiet best.
Not noisily mobbed, and crowded,
Seen thee in flooding light,
Seen thee in perfect calm;
Yet am I sad as at the sight
Of mummy that men embalm.

IONA.

Isle of the past and gone,
The life from thee has departed;
Thy best is now but a carven stone,--
And a memory lonely-hearted!
Yet thou wert a power erewhile,
O'er the great world's mind and heart;
But where now the priests of the Holy Isle
And the skill of its graceful Art?

Skilled was the hand that wrought
Your traceried tombs and crosses,
And silvern brooches that yet are brought
From depths of the black peat mosses;
And theirs was a holy work
Who carried the gospel pure
Where the white waves break by the old White-kirk,
And brought salvation sure.

Was it the Norseman's sword,
And the ships of Thor and Odin
That drove the saints with the sacred Word
From the peaceful ways they trod in?
Was it the Saxon's sway,
Brutal and selfish and strong,
That swept the beautiful Art away,
And stifled the Celtic song?

Only this do we know,
The Celt brought light to the Teuton,
And ever the knowledge of God did grow
In the land he set his foot on;
But as they throve he pined,
But as they smiled he sighed,
But as they grew he surely dwined,
And in their life he died.

O passion of holy love!
O sacrificial people,
Dying to lift men's thoughts above
By altar and cross and steeple!
Through stormy seas ye passed,
And moor and marsh and fen,
To be left behind in the march at last
As weak exhausted men!

They say ye shall rise again
On the level Western prairie,
With a larger life and a keener brain,
Like eagle out of his eyrie;
But not the mind and the heart
That grew by the Lochs and Bens,
Nor the plaintive song and the mystic Art
Nursed in the rushy glens.

The Cry of the Maiden Shareholders.*

Pity us, God! there are five of us here,
   With threescore years on the youngest head,
Five of us sitting in sorrow and fear—
   Well for our widowed one she is dead!
Day and night sitting, we've not laid a head
   Down on a pillow this week and more;
Trembling has seized on us, shrinking and dread,
   To hear the bell ring, or be seen at the door.
      Pity us, pity, O God!

* These Verses appeared in "The Scotsman" newspaper at the time of the failure of the City of Glasgow Bank. And now I reprint them, chiefly because I wish to make grateful acknowledgements to the unknown friends whose generosity enabled me greatly to help those poor ladies till their affairs were finally settled.

Pity us, God! when our father died,
  His mind was at ease, for he left us "shares,"
And a roof o'er our head too; and side by side,
  Happy and loving, we faced life's cares.
Then we were young, but now feeble and old,
  And we never wronged any as far as we knew,
And we tried to do right with our silver and gold,
  And the poor had their portion, the Church had
    its due.
      Pity us, pity, O God!

Pity us, God! we would work if we could,
  But suppler fingers must stitch and hem;
And who would give us our morsel of food,
  Though we span and knitted all day for them?
We never knew work, but to keep ourselves neat,
  And we never knew want, but our wants are small,
And there's bread in the house yet if we could eat,
  But the sickness of sorrow is mixed with it all.
      Pity us, pity, O God!

Pity us, God! must our little things go?
  All—even our mother's things, cherished with care?
Must we leave the old house—the one house that
    we know?
  But not for the poorhouse—Oh, surely not there?

Could they not wait a while?—we will not keep
    them long;
We would live on so little too, cheerful and brave;
But to leave the old house where old memories
    throng
  For the poorhouse, oh! rather the peace of the
    grave,
        Pity us, pity, O God!

Pity us, God! as for those who have wrought
  This terrible ruin so wide and deep,
Oh, how could they do it, and know it not?
  How could they know it, and think or sleep?
But we would not, one of us, change, this day,
  Our lot for theirs, for our hands are clean;
And the bankrupt soul has a darker way
  Than the way of the honest poor ever has been.
        Pity us, pity, O God!

A Cry from the Merse.*

"They have heard evil tidings; there is sorrow on the sea." —
Jerem. xlix., 23.

Half o' us drooned in the Firth ;
   Hearses at ilk ither door !
No a hale heart in the toon,
   No a dry e'e on the shore !
No a hooss but has its dead,
   Father, or cousin, or brither !
For nane o' us stands by himsel',
   We are a' sib to ilk ither.

* In October, 1882, a terrible storm destroyed, in a brief hour, half the boats of the fishers of Eyemouth. This suggested the two poems "From the Merse."

My Janet was wedded to Jake,
  George was my brither-in-law,
Elsie was promised to Will—
  An' noo they're a' dead an' awa';
Drooned within sight o' their hames,
  Throttled richt doon to their graves,
Wi' the screams o' their wives an' the weans
  Mixed up wi' the crash o' the waves.

Lord God, what does it mean?
  They were a' brave lads an' true,
And what can this misery bring
  O' profit tae us or you?
My head gangs roon when I think
  Hoo the sea lay calm in the bay,
Till it had them a' weel in its grip,
  An' took the brave lads for a prey.

Lord, keep me frae sin if ye can:
  I canna be sure what I do;
There's Elsie sits dazed-like an' dumb,
  And Janet moans a' the day through;
I try tae keep hauds o' Thee, Lord,
  But a' that I get for my pains
Is tae drift farther into the dark
  'Mid the wail o' the women an' weans.

A CRY FROM THE MERSE.

Oh, the folk are a' kind in their way,
   Baith gentle an' simple, nae doot;
An' ready wi' pity an' prayers,
   An' siller if siller wu'd do't!
But prayers winna bring the lads back,
   An' pity feels almost like mockin',
An' a' the fine gowd i' the lan'
   Winna sowder the heart that is broken.

The bairnies are greetin' a' day,
   An' the women are moanin' a' nicht,
An' the bread winna gang doon oor throats,
   An' the Book doesna bring ony licht;
An' though there's nae hope in oor hearts,
   We gang an' glower lang at the sea,
An' scan weel the rig o' ilk boat,
   An' then we come hame like tae dee.

Half o' us drooned i' the Firth!
   A' o' us drooned in despair!
Bairns cryin', "Daddie, come hame,"
   As their mithers are rivin' their hair!
An' where there's a corpse they are glad,
   For the sea has the maist in her maw;
An' I watna weel what's tae come neist—
   But, Lord, if ye'd just tak' us a'.

A Remonstrance from the Merse.

Ay! Robin, lad, it's hard to bear,
    An' we've had mony a grief before;
It's nae the first whase yallow hair
    Lay wat and dragglet on the shore.
The sea has gi'en us meat an' bield,
    An' robbed us too o' young an' brave;
But aye we kent, wha ploughed that field
    Was ploughin' o'er an open grave.

We'll see nae mair the bonnie boats
    Trip dainty owre the moon-lit Firth,
Wi' baited lines, or nets an' floats,
    Maist a' oor hard-earned gear on earth:

We'll hear nae mair the lasses gay
    A' daffin' wi' the buirdly chiels,
An' splashin' through the surf and spray
    Tae bring ashore the weel-filled creels.

It's wae and weary is the day,
    An' dark an' dreary is the nicht,
The sunshine o' oor life's away,
    An' stars gi'e but a cauldrife licht.
We lo'ed the Firth, we lo'ed the sea,
    The tanglet rock, the ripply sand,
But noo where'er oor steps may be,
    There's nocht but grief on ilka hand.

Oh, weel I ken your heart is true,
    But, Robin, lad, your words are wild;
An' "laich an' lown" is best for you,
    God hears the breathin' o' a child.
He's no the ane, as I ha'e heard,
    Tae make man an offender be
For naething but a hasty word—
    He leaves that tae the Pharisee:

Yet, Robin, better tae be still,
    An' murmur not, as He has bid;
Wha' wrastles wi' his Maker's will
    Comes hameward lame, as Jacob did.

He made the sea, He sent the win',
   He cast the lift that day in gloom :
Wha judges Him will scarce get in
   Whaur lowly hearts find plenty room.

Speak lown, my man; though God may hear
   The honest thocht that's in the heart,
Folk only catch what meets the ear,
   An' understand it but in part.
Wild thochts will come at times, I ken,
   But then they needna be expressed;
Or say them, lad, tae God, not men;
   They mak' the warst o't, He the best.

Ye canna sowder hearts wi' gowd,
   Nor plaister notes upon your pain;
As little, though ye cry aloud,
   Will that bring back the deid again.
I daurna say its wholly sin
   That ye should wince beneath the rod,
Yet hear the still small voice within,
   Be still and know that this is God.

In Memoriam—Dr. John Brown.

O sweet and pure and tender heart,
   With the child's gift to pray and play,
That, artless in thy perfect art,
Could'st blissful tears to us impart,
   And smile the blissful tears away.

Most human thou of humankind,
   What wealth of love accrued to thee!
To thee dumb creatures looked to find
The meanings which their wistful mind
   Was groping for, and could not see.

We were the better for the mirth,
   We were the better for the tears,

We were the better seeing worth
In the dumb creatures of the earth,
   Their loves, their hatreds, and their fears.

Not all could comprehend thy mirth,
   Thy dainty humour playing round
All things that be; yet heaven and earth
Thine awe and wonder still called forth,
   For all to thee was holy ground.

We are so little; God requires,
   The greatness of His thoughts to prove,
Some altars burning with strange fires,
Some songs not meant for sacred choirs,
   Some souls that shun the common groove.

And thou—thy smile was like a prayer,
   Thy humour like a psalm of praise;
They mingled with the holiest there
Where hearts breathe out their grief and care
   To Him that Ancient is of days.

Yet oftentimes that smile was seen
   Kindling the near edge of a cloud
That gathered o'er thy soul serene,
And haunted thee with anguish keen,
   And bitter wailing low or loud.

That cloud is past of fear and doubt;
  But ah! this other cloud that lies
With hush of silence all about,
And opens to let no man out,
  And hides thee from our wistful eyes!

We gaze at it with brimming tears;
  Vain all our yearning looks and fond;
No smile upon its edge appears;
And yet the faith is wise that hears
  A voice say, It is light beyond.

www.ingramcontent.com/pod-product-compliance
Lightning Source LLC
Chambersburg PA
CBHW032149230426
43672CB00011B/2494